BEYOND THE
GREAT DIVIDE

BEYOND THE GREAT DIVIDE

HOW A NATION BECAME
A NEIGHBORHOOD

GOVERNOR
GEORGE PATAKI

WITH TREY RADEL

Post Hill
PRESS

Post Hill Press
New York • Nashville
posthillpress.com

TABLE OF CONTENTS

INTRODUCTION

WHY NOW?

Why would I, a former governor and presidential candidate, write a book *now*, sharing my experiences, my reflections, and my vision for this country?

Let me assure you: I am not running for any political office. Nor will I use this book to grandstand or settle scores. This book is beyond politics. It is personal, well intentioned, and comes from the depths of my heart.

I was governor of New York for twelve years, including on September 11, 2001. Here, for the first time, I will share the events of that day, as well as the devastation and recovery from it, *from my perspective*. I will take you inside that fateful day, sharing stories of heroism, total chaos, brave men and women who gave all, and utter heartbreak.

Beyond the attacks, I hope to bring people together to reflect on what came out of the pain and suffering in those horrific days after 9/11. Like the mythological phoenix, America rose from the ashes, with our people bonded like never before—a truly *United* States of America. Americans came together as strong as ever in my lifetime. Now, the country is divided as it hasn't been in more than a hundred years.

I'm writing because I am concerned about the future of our great country. I'm writing because of my love for this country. I'm writing to reflect on what was—and what can be.

In sharing my perspective of where we are today, politically and culturally, and through the lens of the September 11 attacks, I hope to shed light on what I call "the great divide." It's a divide not just between left and right or Republicans and Democrats, but quite simply between the American people and their government. This division has fostered anger and resentment toward Washington and among Americans toward one another.

A huge part of the divide comes from legislation sold to us, the American public, year after year, *based on false pretenses*. Two monumental decisions, one each from Republican and Democratic administrations, are embedded in foreign and domestic policy. We'll get to those.

Across the political spectrum, people look at Washington and ask, "Does this government reflect my views? Is this government acting in the interest of the American people?" I fear that saying yes to those questions is getting more and more difficult. Self-serving politicians are simply seeking partisan advantage for their own power and prestige, and Americans are paying the price.

Having led the liberal Democratic state of New York for three terms as a conservative Republican governor, I have drawn on my experiences and will share ideas as to how we as Americans can reclaim our future *together*. Just as the wreckage of Ground Zero and Lower Manhattan has been rebuilt into a soaring, unifying tribute, I am confident that our faith in Washington and in our democracy can be rebuilt to even greater heights.

We were as united as ever after 9/11; we can unite again.

America, for all of its faults and turbulent history, is like no other country in the history of humankind—united in the concept that we are all one, sharing the same common destiny. And if we close the great divide, our future will be filled with opportunity and hope.

PROLOGUE

Federal Hall, New York City
September 2002

"WE WOULD LIKE TO THANK YOU FOR YOUR SUPPORT OF THIS RESOLUTION," Congressman Charles Rangel said, and we listened raptly, "that gives us in New York an opportunity to say thank you."

It was September 6, 2002, one year after terrorists had crashed planes into the World Trade Center towers, killing thousands of men, women, and children. To mark the day, Congress formally gathered at Federal Hall in Lower Manhattan. The historical Federal Hall is where George Washington was sworn in as president, and before that, where American colonists met to draft a protest letter to Britain saying, "No taxation without representation." In two hundred years, this was only the second time lawmakers had convened outside of Washington, DC. The first time was 1987 in Philadelphia, when Congress commemorated the two hundredth anniversary of the creation of the United States House and Senate.

As Charlie stood at the podium with a massive American flag draped behind him, my fellow New Yorker's words, delivery, and passion pulled at my heartstrings. Charlie, typically one of the most partisan politicians in the country, was so moving that I smiled broadly as he spoke. You might think it odd that I reflect on something so simple as a smile. But you have to understand that after those horrific terror attacks, directed at the state in which I was serving as governor and at the country I love, every day of the previous year had been a roller coaster of emotions. I was sad at times, occasionally angry, but always optimistic. And like so many others, I was exhausted yet unwavering and determined.

Charlie continued, thanking the Republican administration.

"Thank you for the way you responded to the attack on our city and our state, to give our mayor and our governor an opportunity to be here on this historic event to say you didn't treat us like New Yorkers, you treated us like Americans."

Charlie, and other members of Congress from New York who spoke after him, reflected on how the country had come together for the city. We were all one. We were all Americans.

That was then.

Today, we are the Divided Tribes of America, bound by party labels. For many, politics has replaced religion. We worship at the altar of cable-news networks, where pundits are priests, preaching the same talking points every day. We lock ourselves in echo chambers of social media, where devout followers lift us up or tear us down depending on what side we're on. There's no conversation, no empathy, no understanding. There are men and women unbreakable in their beliefs who will do everything they can to break you into submitting to their political doctrine. In the last few years, we have witnessed political fanatics use violence and, even worse, watched our elected leaders in Congress incite and encourage it.

In June of 2018, Representative Maxine Waters, one of the most powerful and longest-serving Democratic members of the House of Representatives, told people to gang up on anyone who worked with the Trump administration. "If you see anybody from that cabinet in a restaurant, in a department store, at a gasoline station," she said, "you get out and you create a crowd, and you push back on them, and you tell them they're not welcome anymore, anywhere."

She added, "History will record that, while he tried to step on all of us, we kicked him in his rear and we stepped on him."

A few months later, former Attorney General Eric Holder, the man once in charge of the Department of Justice, said, "When they go low, we kick 'em."

The rhetoric is one thing; the very real acts of violence are another. White supremacists murdered a woman during a "Unite the Right" rally in Charlottesville, Virginia. An avowed Bernie Sanders supporter unloaded an assault rifle in an attempt to assassinate a large group of House and Senate Republicans who were playing baseball, practicing for a charity game.

Are these news reports from our great country or from some violent third-world country?

The attacks of September 11 united us in incredibly strong ways as Americans. We dealt with pain, suffering, and consequences, but families healed and the economy recovered. It's the political fallout that plagues us today. In the years thereafter, American political culture fractured along ideology and party lines and drifted into the great divide. Today, our society seems to be as divided as in the Civil War era, separated by political tribes that demand ideological purity coupled with blind loyalty.

How did this happen? How did a country, unified like never before in my lifetime on September 12, 2001, become so dangerously divided? More important, what can we do about it? How can we reclaim our understanding that we are all in this together?

CHAPTER 1

THE ONLY THING WE HAVE
TO FEAR IS FEAR ITSELF

New York City
September 11, 2001, 8:58 a.m.

"Dad, did you see what happened? A plane just hit the World Trade Center!"

It was my oldest daughter, Emily, calling. "What?" I asked incredulously, even though I'd heard every word she said.

"A plane hit one of the towers. They're evacuating now."

As the governor of New York, I rarely stayed in New York City. I lived in Garrison with my wife, Libby, and our four young kids. Albany, the state capital—an hour and a half north of where we lived—was where I spent most of my long workdays. But today, of all days in our nation's history, was an exception.

On that fateful day, September 11, 2001, Libby and I happened to be sleeping at a friend's place on the Upper East Side of Manhattan, about ten miles north of the towers downtown. My daughter was working at Bloomberg News in Midtown.

CHAPTER 1

Out of instinct, I stood up and shot over to the window. It was a beautiful day. I peeked my head out but couldn't see that far south. I grabbed the remote and turned on the TV.

There it was, the North Tower on fire, with news anchors sharing the little they knew. Some speculated that it was a small to midsize plane that had gone off course, or maybe the pilot had had a medical emergency.

How little they knew. How little any of us knew.

As I watched the tower burn, I, like the news anchor, wondered the same. Was this some sort of colossal, fatal mistake? Was it a mechanical failure?

With my daughter still on the phone, we both remained silent watching the live news coverage.

"Dad, has this happened before? How?"

I could hear a touch of panic in my daughter's voice. I tried to calm her. "It must be some sort of freak, terrible accident, but Emily, I'm sure the fire department is already working it. They'll get people out of there."

My eyes remained fixated on the TV. Something deep inside of me was saying this was no accident. With my quick glance out the window, I had seen it was a crystal-clear morning. A plane doesn't just fly into one of the world's tallest buildings on a day like that. *Something was wrong.* Yet I told my adult daughter, still my little girl, "Everything will be fine."

Instinctively, I thought everything might *not* be fine.

Then I saw the second plane hit.

As I did, I thought about Emily; my two sons, Owen and Teddy; and my youngest daughter, Allison. Then I thought about the victims downtown who were perishing—on live TV. I thought about the first responders heading up those infinite steps of the World Trade Center.

Only later would it dawn on me to think about more than my family and New Yorkers. The entire world was about to change dramatically, and it was happening in my city and state.

CHAPTER 2

I BELIEVE IN AN AMERICA THAT IS ON THE MARCH—AN AMERICA RESPECTED BY ALL NATIONS, FRIENDS, AND FOES ALIKE

BEFORE SEPTEMBER 11, THE UNITED STATES LOOKED AND FELT A little naïve, but not in a negative way. Quite the opposite. The US was a bit starry-eyed, unaffected by negativity around the world and rather unpretentious. Compared to even the wealthiest nations of Western Europe, our previous couple of centuries were relatively free of domestic or foreign terrorism. There had been no threats of military coups or dictatorships, as so many other countries had struggled with throughout the twentieth century. No. In fact, we were vibrant, energetic, and happy. The United States was full of peace and prosperity, all of it built on something quintessentially American: *unabashed, unbridled optimism.*

Old Europe looked at us with envy, almost lovingly, like an innocent sibling. Many parts of the world gazed at us with admiration, others with jealousy and anger.

CHAPTER 2

> **I, George E. Pataki, do solemnly swear that I will support the Constitution of the United States and the Constitution of the State of New York...**
>
> —upon assuming the office of governor of New York, January 1, 1995

Six years before 9/11, I was sworn in as the fifty-third governor of the State of New York. I defeated popular liberal icon and three-term Democratic Governor Mario Cuomo, and I won as a Republican. My win wasn't just out of the ordinary in Democrat-dominated New York; it was a huge upset.

The year was 1995. Brad Pitt was *People* magazine's Sexiest Man Alive. Coolio rocked the radio charts. *Seinfeld* and *Friends* dominated television. *Braveheart* won Best Picture. For the few who had them, cell phones were used only for calls. And if you didn't know how to do the Macarena, you were a communist!

Undoubtedly, there were some serious issues boiling under America's skin. O. J. Simpson's murder trial captivated people from around the world, highlighting some of our country's racial tensions. In April of that year, Timothy McVeigh bombed a federal building in Oklahoma City. Only two years prior, Islamic extremists had detonated a bomb under the North Tower of the World Trade Center.

Even with these horrific events, America's spirit could not be broken. As the sons and daughters of immigrants and of those who had conquered the frontier, we have optimism running deep in our DNA. I know this as a second-generation immigrant. What my father instilled in me comes from generations of belief that we will climb over the next hill, conquer the next frontier, and know that our children's lives will be better than ours.

While there has been, and always will be, strife and tough issues to deal with, the reality is that America was full of its inherent optimism before 9/11. We still believed in our institutions, our churches, our universities, and yes, our government, regardless of which party controlled Congress. America was built on optimism and the same confidence I felt when taking office. And as an eternal optimist, I hoped to inspire others.

Sure, our country has had plenty of ups and downs, long periods of turmoil as well as dark chapters in our history. But the modern America that emerged was one full of hope. Our people got along really well, even with a history of the evils of slavery, racial strife, and questionable domestic and foreign policy decisions over the decades. We could have civil conversations with one another. Whether politicians on the House floor or political polar opposites at our own homes over a family meal, we could share ideas. We could disagree without being disagreeable.

My election reflected that. I ended up serving three conservative terms as a Republican governor in an overwhelmingly Democratic state. Plus, we got stuff done!

Before my swearing in, I sat down with my opponent, soon-to-be-former-Governor Cuomo. While we had profound political differences on everything from taxes to crime, we talked at length about our state's issues in a cordial conversation. That day, Mario shared only one piece of advice with me: "Move your offices out of the World Trade Center and into Midtown. Everything happens in Midtown." He was right. Meetings and media events were typically held somewhere south of Central Park (that is, below Fifty-Ninth Street) and north of about Thirty-Fourth Street. A few years later, we moved our offices to Midtown. I still wonder if I would have been in the World Trade Center office that morning. Thank you, Mario.

* * *

THE THREE PRESIDENTS LEADING UP TO 9/11—RONALD REAGAN, George H. W. Bush, and Bill Clinton—were great examples of leaders who knew how to get things done. Each had a Congress controlled by the other party, yet they knew how to work across the aisle. They also understood the art of *compromise* and had the audacity to believe that it was not a dirty word! It was Ronald Reagan, the high priest of conservatism, who said, "The person who agrees with you eighty percent of the time is a friend and an ally, not a twenty percent traitor." These were the types of people I could work with.

President Clinton understood compromise well. He often reflected on what our forefathers wanted and how to apply their philosophy practically. "Our constitution was designed by people who were idealistic but not ideological," he once said. "There's a big difference. You can have a philosophy that tends to be liberal or conservative but still be open to evidence, experience, and argument. That enables people with honest differences to find practical, principled compromise." On this, Clinton got it. While it wasn't always pretty, he worked with a domineering Republican Congress, led by House Speaker Newt Gingrich. During Clinton's tenure, Democrats and Republicans passed welfare-reform measures and kept debt and deficits in check.

Those three presidents, Reagan, H. W. Bush, and Clinton, knew how to get things done, politically and practically. Another common trait they all shared was a sense of optimism, an undying belief in America. These men knew America. They believed in America. More important, they led others to believe.

As awful as the September 11 attacks were, in the aftermath, the country was more unified than ever before. Patriotism was in! For about a year, on any given street corner, in any local pub, you could hear random chants of "USA! USA!" or people singing "God Bless America." American flags were selling so fast that stores couldn't keep them in stock, even with the millions being shipped in from China. The American flag was a hot-ticket item on T-shirts, shorts, underwear, bras, bikinis, earrings, and more, and as a tattoo. President George W. Bush had sky-high approval ratings.

A few years later, though, the unity began to fracture as questionable political decisions followed—domestic and foreign. The great divide took hold. The divide cut across cultural and political lines. President Bush's team set a tone of "you're either with us or against us." While this may have been an appropriate reference to the new global War on Terror, it would soon take hold in the American psyche. As we descended into two wars, in Afghanistan and Iraq, the members of the public became increasingly distrustful of government and of one another. That hot new fad of unity and patriotism began to fade.

With our patriotic honeymoon over, a nasty partisanship was injected into politics and our culture in a way rarely seen in modern times. Year after year, the "with us or against us" attitude began to seep into American society, and quickly, we took sides. You were either Republican or Democrat. You were either for the Iraq War or not. You were either a patriot or a hater.

Have you seen this quote? "Every nation has to either be with us or against us."

Who said it? Spoiler: it wasn't Bush.

One of the most powerful and prominent Democrats in the nation spoke those words on September 13, 2001. It was then-New York Senator Hillary Clinton.

Only days later, in a joint session of Congress, President George W. Bush conveyed the same sentiment: "Every nation, in every region, now has a decision to make. Either you are with us, or you are with the terrorists."

President Bush set this tone the moment he launched US military forces into Afghanistan. At that time, Democrats and Republicans were solidly united behind him. So was the American public. We also had the support of almost the entire globe.

Then came Iraq.

As the country was deep into two wars, the public began to divide based on policy disagreements almost exclusively related to foreign policy. Elected Democrats and Republicans in Washington upped their rhetoric. They turned policy disagreements into personal battles.

For a full year after 9/11, America had a fleeting moment of unity we had not had since the bombing of Pearl Harbor or the assassination of JFK. But it deteriorated; it all fell apart.

What happened?

Today the "with us or against us" attitude is more present than ever before. But it's not directed toward countries like France or Turkey. It's aimed directly at our fellow Americans. From petty, manufactured culture wars to genuine policy disagreements, everything has become *us versus them*. American versus American. And the world watches in disbelief.

Optimism has turned into pessimism. Civility has turned into toxicity.

> terrorism (noun)—the unlawful use of violence and intimidation, especially against civilians, in the pursuit of political aims.
>
> —*Oxford English Dictionary*

The aims of the terrorists who attacked us that day went far beyond bringing down buildings; they wanted to bring down the American way of life. They were aiming to disrupt, anger, and break up a unified, resolute society that believed in freedom and democracy. They wanted chaos and distrust to rain down from the highest levels of government and permeate its people. In the months after 9/11, their plans didn't materialize. They backfired. America remained resolute and unified.

Years later, though, distrust, anger, and resentment began to permeate the American public like a broken relationship. Our unity, our love, our companionship, and most unfortunately, our optimism disintegrated.

Looking at America today, with its great divide sapping American confidence, coupled with hate bred by political leaders, I ask: *Did the terrorists win?*

This is a question no one in public service dares ask or speak of. Abroad and here at home, we are struggling with policy, politics, and culture. We are more divided then ever in my lifetime. While no factions have broken out into war, supporters—or better said, fanatics—on both sides of the aisle have used violence to achieve their goals.

Domestically, politicians stoke hatred. They spout off extreme rhetoric and use politics to divide our people in order to win policy debates, campaigns, and culture wars. The terrorists wanted to throw our country into chaos and divide us as a society, and vapid, ignorant politicians have inadvertently become their foot soldiers.

The terrorists initiated division in our country. State actors from around the world, namely Russia, continue to add fuel to the fire. They directly target Americans through social media propaganda, hacks, and leaks. They boldly and openly work to influence our elections, not through collusion but through division. They polarize the public with "useful idiots," to use Joseph Stalin's term, all doing their dirty work and tearing our great country apart.

We, as Americans, must ask ourselves: Will we allow these evil outside forces, trying to destroy us from within, continue to divide us? Or can we recognize them, stand up to them, and use them as an inspiration to unify us once again?

CHAPTER 3

IF TYRANNY AND OPPRESSION COME TO THIS LAND, IT WILL BE IN THE GUISE OF FIGHTING A FOREIGN ENEMY

New York City
September 11, 2001, 9:03 a.m.

BANG! FLAMES SHOT OUT OF THE SOUTH TOWER.

It happened again. A second plane.

Without saying a word, I began pacing, eyes still fixated on the TV. In times of crisis, when things get even more chaotic, I find myself getting calmer, more collected, and focused. You have to strike a balance between thinking and acting. If you overthink the situation, nothing gets done. Act too quickly and you risk reckless decisions. You need to understand the nature of the challenge and come up with solutions to deal with it as quickly as possible.

This challenge, though, got infinitely more horrifying.

The news station cued the seconds-old footage back up. This time, the world watched a second massive plane barrel directly into the other tower in slow motion.

Right there. Right then. I knew.

With Libby in the room and a state trooper in the hallway, I firmly whispered to myself, "This is intentional. This is a terror attack."

Immediately, I called New York City Mayor Rudolph Giuliani. "Rudy, I'm in the city now. I'm going to call up the National Guard and activate the state's emergency response team. Let me know anything you need."

Activating that team would initiate mutual aid, which meant all hands on deck across the state. I knew how grave the situation was going to be, based simply on what I was watching on TV. I knew we'd need everything, because the loss of life was going to be catastrophic. There was no doubt in my mind.

Rudy was quick and to the point. "Fine and thank you, George. We'll stay in touch."

He was calm, but I could hear concern in his voice. The conversation ended quickly. We had no idea what was in store for us, but we both knew there was a monumental task ahead of us that would require steady leadership.

The morning of September 11, 2001, began with shock and continued with horror.

In the minutes that followed, Rudy became the bold and brave face of 9/11. Weeks later, he became affectionately known as "America's Mayor." In fact, he would come back to me with a request to hold on to that title in an unprecedented way. It was something I didn't expect, even from a former prosecutor-turned-shrewd politician.

His request, Rudy's request, which we'll get to later, made me realize one of the immediate consequences of 9/11: everything we believed in as Americans—law and order, culture and traditions—would be up for grabs.

As soon as I got off the phone with the mayor, I activated the National Guard and all of our emergency responders. Then I called the Albany Command Center, where the heads of the emergency responding teams had all come together.

"Get me the president."

Minutes later, I was on the phone with President George W. Bush. He had been at the job less than a year as commander in chief of the United States of America, which was now directly under attack.

"Mr. President, I understand you're aware of the situation. I have a request."

President Bush was walking out of an elementary school in the sleepy beach community of Sarasota, Florida. During his short stay there, he had been briefed that one plane had hit the World Trade Center. With few details, many assumed it was an accident. Then, as he picked up *The Pet Goat* to read to second graders, Andy Card, his chief of staff, leaned over and whispered in his ear, "A second plane hit the second tower. America is under attack."

When the president took my call, my request was simple, but I knew it would have a massive effect. "Sir, I'm requesting you shut down the airspace over New York City." For all the horror we were seeing, no one knew what might be coming next.

President Bush, who had been on the job for eight months, was often ridiculed by the press as being ill-equipped to handle the grave responsibilities of the presidency. He gave me his answer—his ominous, foreboding, calm answer: "Pataki, I just shut down air traffic over the entire country."

His answer sent chills down my spine. At that moment, I knew this was something much bigger. I wondered what else he knew at the time. Thoughts raced through my mind. As two New York landmarks burned and innumerable people perished, I knew the entire country was under some sort of orchestrated attack.

The president then boarded Air Force One. He told me, "I'm heading west to pick up military escorts. I'll call you from the plane." Our call ended, but we'd talk again soon.

There were all sorts of issues that President Bush had to address from the sky that morning, and to this day, I'm not sure the American public knows what he was going through in those hours after the attack. He was criticized sharply for not returning to Washington,

DC, or finding some way to take to the airwaves and address the American people. But the decision was out of his hands.

To protect the president and the vice president, the Secret Service uses code words when discussing them over radio, phone, or in person. They do the same for places, locations, and objects like Air Force One. That morning, intelligence had intercepted some foreign actors using the secret words for Air Force One. President Bush wanted to go back to the White House, but the Secret Service, backed up by credible threats that intelligence agencies had received, said no. The president didn't have a choice.

The president flew west from Florida and picked up his fighter escorts. He called me again to check in and get new information. This call was brief. He relayed some more information on shutting down airline traffic and how the federal government was responding. As our conversation began to wrap up, the phone connection began to cut in and out. Remember, this was 2001. Even though the president had top-of-the-line communications equipment in the plane, the call was still breaking up. In the chaos, with the line cutting in and out, he wrapped up by saying something that came through crystal clear: "Pataki, now I understand what they mean by the fog of war."

As I heard the president use the word "war," chills once again ran down my spine.

Back to the TV, still in the apartment.

I watched as the towers continued to burn on live television. I needed to get to them. It was now my job to do whatever I could to help provide the state's support to the thousands of first responders who were descending upon Lower Manhattan. It was now my job to help secure and save as many lives as possible. It was now my job to bring stability and comfort through leadership to one of the most densely populated cities in America and one of the most populous states in the country.

I geared up to leave. Then…

"Oh, my God!"

The towers fell, first the South Tower at 9:59 a.m., then the North Tower at 10:28 a.m. Steel and concrete crumbled like grains of sand running through an hourglass.

"No!"

How many innocent men and women perished? How many fire-fighters, police officers, and paramedics just died? More personally, how many people did I know in those towers?

My heart sank. My stomach turned.

It wasn't even eleven o'clock in the morning and already the World Trade Center towers had crumbled to the ground after terrorists rammed two commercial airliners through them. Another plane shot like a missile into the Pentagon in Washington, DC, and a fourth crashed into the ground outside Shanksville, Pennsylvania. Air traffic throughout the country was shut down. The skies were silent. And before my very eyes, thousands of people lost their lives as the country's two tallest buildings came crashing down.

America was under attack, starting with my beloved state of New York, which I represented, served, and led as governor.

With massive plumes of smoke rising over Manhattan, I sat down. I watched. Then I closed my eyes, bowed my head, and said a prayer. A state trooper walked in, snapping me back into the moment.

"Sir, Colonel Wiese is on his way. He is flying in via helicopter to the East Thirty-Fourth Street Heliport."

Lieutenant Colonel Dan Wiese headed up my security detail, and with his cropped hair, intense stare, and thin, athletic build, he looked every bit the part. I called him Danny. As he was the head of my security team, we were together almost 24/7. I could always count on him to look out for my safety. Even in the most mundane situations—for example, doing a meet and greet with constituents—Danny was right there hovering nearby, not only scoping out the scene and everything around us, but always, and I mean always, looking at people's hands. It's exactly what he was trained to do—to stay on guard and look for someone pulling something out or trying to attack. Danny was a trusted friend and partner, with me almost every waking minute of every day. To my wife and children, he was like family.

On the night of September 10, Danny slept at his home in Garrison, New York. He had been working long hours in Albany preparing security for an upcoming event. Garrison now was out; getting to Manhattan was in.

Somehow, the always resourceful Danny commandeered a helicopter after top brass in the state police told him no one was flying a thing because airspace over the city—and country—was shut down. Danny basically told them, "Screw you; this is a state police helicopter that's clearly marked. We're flying it to Manhattan right now. I'm going to go get the governor."

The trooper still in the room with me added, "Governor, he'll assist in bringing you north to Albany."

"Albany?" I fired back.

"Yes, sir. We'll take you direct to the command post there."

Before he finished his sentence, I was shaking my head. "No. I'm not leaving."

"Governor, we have to get you out of the city for your security now."

"No way. We're going to the office in Midtown."

With Manhattan being such an enormous and critical part of the state, economically and culturally, the governor always has an office in the city. I was steadfast and said again, "That's where we are going first."

First—because I knew we would head to the site of the World Trade Center eventually, regardless of how horrific the scene was.

"Sir?" the trooper asked in disbelief.

"Get a car ready. We're heading to Midtown."

For the first time in my career, after six years of heeding my security detail's advice loyally, I refused their request. *No way.* Of course, I knew exactly what they wanted and why. They were desperately concerned for my safety, and they were right. I'd be safer in Albany, 150 miles away from Manhattan. There, I could go to the Emergency Command Center, where the heads of first responders and emergency command officials had come together to react and plan, meeting in an underground shelter that had been built to withstand nuclear bombs.

Sadly, in my many years serving as governor, I had enormous experience with serious tragedies. I witnessed some of the most terrifying situations a human being can go through. I also watched bighearted people step up to help during some of the most awful moments in life.

There were the large-scale wildfires that ripped through the Pine Barrens, a publicly protected nature reserve, which threatened to burn down populated residential areas on the east end of Long Island. Shortly after, the Great Ice Storm of 1998 hit the Adirondacks hard, knocking out power for weeks in the dead of winter. Lives were lost. And then, in one of the worst events prior to 9/11, there was TWA Flight 800 that crashed shortly after taking off from JFK airport. All 230 people on board died.

In every tragedy, I learned the importance of *presence*. I saw how much it meant to people to simply be there, to comfort those who had lost loved ones or publicly address problems and work toward solutions. In times of crisis, you do not leave the affected area. You stay. This moment called for presence and leadership, not a retreat upstate away from Manhattan.

In some way, those terrible moments during my time as governor served as my training ground for 9/11. It was a sad reflection of what I had been through, but when those buildings came crashing down, instinctively I knew what needed to be done. I needed to stay in Manhattan, and when the time was right, when I would not be a burden or distraction to first responders, I would go to the World Trade Center. There was no way I was heading to Albany. I was going to get downtown, directly to the towers, or at least the area where they once stood.

"Sir, we're ready."

Before we left, I called Emily and told her to meet me at my office in Midtown.

Troopers had two Suburbans on standby outside the front door. One was for me; the other was for Libby. Though I worried about friends I had in the World Trade Center, I took solace in knowing my family was safe. It may have been selfish, but it was a very real feeling. My daughter Emily would soon be on her way to meet me, and Libby would go home. We were quickly escorted out of the apartment. Everything was moving so fast, but in that moment, as we arrived at the cars, time slowed as I embraced Libby. I held her tight.

"I love you. Tell the kids I love them. Hug them for me."

Troopers whisked her away. She headed north to get the rest of the kids out of school. Every school in the state shut down and sent the children home.

Now out of the apartment, where I had been fixated on the TV, I noticed that things were suddenly peaceful. As my mind slowed, I inhaled a deep breath of the cool September air. I looked left. I looked right. You could hear sirens in the distance, a common sound in the city, but other than that, there was an eerie silence. Amazingly, in Manhattan, one of the most congested and densely packed places in the world, there were no cars. The roads were empty.

"Sir!"

My moment of peace was broken. I looked at my security team, and they quickly ushered me into the SUV. As soon as my seat belt clicked, the driver slammed on the gas. *Vroom!* My head jerked back. We began flying down the streets and avenues of Manhattan like the chase scene in *The French Connection.*

As we cut sharp corners and accelerated, I picked up the car phone to try to get Mayor Giuliani back on the line. I had no luck. I would later learn that he was trapped in a building that had its doors and most exits covered by the debris of the World Trade Center buildings after they fell.

We headed directly to the office at 633 Third Avenue, which was a good fifty blocks away from where we were, but still way north of downtown. There, I would meet critical staff members, coordinate a response, and also connect with my daughter Emily, who left her office at Bloomberg News in Midtown to meet me.

As we headed south on Park Avenue, I saw for the first time in person the disturbing sight, which remains seared in my mind today. I looked out the front window. The massive towers that always had been visible were gone. Huge clouds of thick, white smoke rose over Lower Manhattan. My heart dropped. Seeing it for the first time in person, I was crushed. All I could think about was how many people, how many of my friends—people I'd given jobs to or worked with in the towers—had died. I wondered how many police officers and firefighters who weren't even in the WTC towers that morning charged directly in and ran up the infinite staircases only to meet their demise. Impossibly, my heart sank lower.

Seeing this also reaffirmed why I was not going to the site of the attacks right away. There would be a time, but not now. The last thing I wanted emergency responders worrying about was some politician or dignitary they had to protect, attend to, or even feel obligated to talk to. They needed to focus on their job: saving lives. Me too. I needed to coordinate the response and lead in this time of crisis.

As I was staring at the massive columns of smoke rising over Manhattan and dwarfing our city's skyscrapers, another human instinct kicked in: fear—not for me but for our city and our country. As the SUV continued to speed ahead, I began to look closely at every building and each and every person on the sidewalk. My mind raced. *What's going to happen next? Would there be another terror attack?*

As we arrived at my office, I pulled my mind back into the moment. I mentally made a list of people I would need to call and the executive orders I would need to issue. Decisions, big decisions, had to be made. The vehicle stopped. I got out and quickly made my way toward the building. There, Danny, who had just flown in by helicopter, met me at the doors. Before I could speak, he said, "You shouldn't be here, Governor." He wasn't patronizing. Danny was concerned for my safety and the welfare of the state should something happen to me.

"What now? What's the issue *here*?" I demanded to know.

"The UN, sir."

The United Nations building was nearby; top security officials from Washington and Albany were convinced it was also a target. Danny was merely relaying the intel and suggestions he had received: "You should leave now."

After breaking my tradition of always heeding security's suggestions only a half hour ago, I did it again. "No. I'm sorry, Danny. I have to be here."

He nodded. He didn't need to say anything else. Neither did I. After the years we had spent together in sometimes dangerous and uncertain places and situations, he knew why I would stay. He recognized the importance of what we were doing and why. He turned to walk with me into the building and head up to the office.

I was soon situated at my desk. Key staff members came in to help us mount our response, and I worked the phones. A call came in from Deputy Mayor Rudy Washington, one that made me both concerned and confident.

"Governor, in the absence of the mayor, I'm making decisions right now."

God, I hope Rudy Giuliani's okay, I thought.

The deputy mayor continued: "We went ahead and set up Gracie Mansion as a temporary command center, a base to organize and make decisions."

Gracie Mansion is the official residence of the mayor of New York. It's located at Eighty-Eighth Street and FDR Drive. It's way north of downtown and the site of the World Trade Center. What is downtown, though, is city hall, and that was not an option for the deputy mayor or other city leaders.

Later that day, when I finally spoke to Mayor Giuliani and learned he was okay, he let me know that his command center in 7 World Trade Center had been destroyed. He had made the decision to locate a new temporary command center for the city in the New York City Police Academy on East Twentieth Street. When he told me that, I made what was one of the most important decisions that day—to bring my entire operation with me to the same location. Our state command center was located in Albany. That morning, we used our Midtown offices. And then, that afternoon, we moved all state staff to the academy as well. All of us, city and state personnel, set up in the same room at the same tables. Later that evening, when people from the Federal Emergency Management Agency (FEMA) arrived, they also located their operations in the same room.

Every day, as we went through our emergency responses, we coordinated efficiently and effectively. There were no gaps in response; there was no miscommunication. When Rudy talked to me, his commissioners knew exactly what they were responsible for and so did my team. No one ever had a doubt who was responsible for what. Unlike the situation with Hurricane Katrina, there was never any finger pointing among city, state, or federal officials.

But back on the phone at my desk in Midtown earlier, Deputy Mayor Washington continued, "Governor, you and I can communicate from here on out. Anything you need, you let us know. Any suggestions you have, I'm open."

"And the same to you. I'm here for you."

One of the first things I did from the apartment was to ask for units of the National Guard to come into New York City and for state police to create a perimeter around the World Trade Center complex. We wanted only first responders and others who were necessary to help rescue people at the site. We barred everyone else. We didn't want do-gooders or civilian heroes, and we sure as hell didn't want gawkers. The area was dangerous, and there was *still* a concern about more attacks.

From the office, I began making decisions that had enormous impacts on the city and beyond. We shut down all bridges and tunnels in and out of the city. We made sure the Emergency Command Center in Albany was on the highest alert and functioning at full capacity. I activated mutual aid. This allowed fire stations from anywhere in the state to come and assist in Manhattan. Eventually, we called in crews from as far out as Binghamton, which is 185 miles away from the city, as well as fire companies from out of state. Every firefighter from all of the five boroughs descended on Lower Manhattan that day. As they did, other fire stations moved in to backfill for those firehouses. I was on multiple calls at the same time, with one phone to each ear, talking to different agencies. A disturbing sight snapped me out of executive mode, though.

As I hung up the phone, getting ready to organize our next steps, I heard the people in the office gasp. I looked up. In walked Eliot Spitzer, the attorney general of New York. My mouth dropped. *Spitzer was covered head to toe in white, chalk-like ash.* You could make out his eyes and some of his face, but his body was covered in a thick, white film of soot. He looked like a ghost. He had run and then walked all the way from his office downtown to mine, nearly four miles, escaping the horror of the site.

Once again, I was witnessing something I had never before seen in person. Gazing at him, I was horrified and mesmerized. "My God," was all I could get out.

"Governor," he said, his voice trembling.

I walked out from behind my desk, approached him, and we embraced. It was all we could do. There were no words. There was nothing to say. Immediately, any political issues we'd had with each other in the past became nonexistent.

He briefed me on what he had witnessed, what he had been through, and how he ran as the towers came crashing down. It was shocking to hear it firsthand.

As that emotional moment wrapped up, another one began. My daughter walked in.

"Emily," I said loudly, so relieved to see her in person. In that second, she was my world. I hugged her like never before. I held her tight.

"I love you, Dad."

"I love you too."

I also reassured her, letting her know everything was going to be okay.

Let's be honest, though. I didn't know everything was going to be okay, but I would fight like hell to make sure it was—for my daughter, my family miles away, the millions of people in Manhattan at that hour, and their family members around the world witnessing what was happening on the news *in real time.*

Danny walked back into the room. "Sir, we're ready."

It was time to start our journey downtown.

We hopped in the SUV and darted south. First, we stopped at Saint Vincent's Hospital on Twelfth Street in Greenwich Village, a few blocks north of the towers. As it was a prominent hospital near the World Trade Center, doctors and nurses there stood ready to help save as many lives as possible and care for the injured. Danny hopped out of the car. I followed. Outside the hospital, gurneys lined the street as far as you could see. Doctors, nurses, and staff all stood there waiting for the injured.

Sadly, the hundreds, potentially thousands, of injured patients would never arrive. They died when the towers came down. Those who escaped did so mostly unharmed.

Those gurneys would remain outside. Empty.

There were a few patients inside. I went in and spoke to victims who either had evacuated the towers or run while the towers collapsed. It was heart-wrenching and heartwarming. These were the survivors, the few who made it. As I shook hands with a few of them and was about to leave, I was jarred by a woman's voice behind me.

"Governor Pataki."

In those two words, I could hear sadness and desperation. I turned and looked. It was Christy Ferer, the wife of my friend and trusted partner Neil Levin. Only months before, I appointed Neil to head up the Port Authority as its executive director. The Port Authority owned and operated the towers. Its offices were in them.

"Governor, have you heard from Neil?" she asked, her voice cracking, unsteady with fear. "You have to find Neil."

"Where was he last, Christy?" I asked. My heart dropped yet again when she told me.

"Windows on the World."

Neil had a breakfast meeting that morning at the restaurant Windows on the World in the North Tower, the first tower to be hit. I knew the restaurant well. I had held countless events there and attended many others. It was on the 106th floor, well above where the plane had hit. Christy was hysterical, desperate to know if he had made it out alive.

The morning had already been an emotional roller coaster from hell, but this was different. This was a close, personal friend. I had known Christy and Neil for years. I embraced her.

"Christy, I don't know. I haven't heard from him, but I know firefighters are doing everything they can."

I thought about Neil. We'd had lunch together the week before to talk about the future of the Port Authority. While I had my doubts about his survival, I held out hope, like so many others around the world who knew people in the towers.

Maybe he was able to evacuate, or maybe he canceled his meeting, I thought, knowing that was probably not the case.

All of us who knew someone in New York on 9/11 so desperately hoped we'd hear a loved one's voice on the phone: "Hey, I'm okay!" Or see a mother, father, brother, or sister walk through the door again: "I made it out!"

Sadly, that would not be the case with Neil.

I hugged Christy again, letting her know I was heading to the site and would do everything I could to find him and contact her. The next time we saw each other was at a memorial service for Neil a week later.

By the time I left the hospital, reporters and cameras hovered around the area, also waiting for patients to be brought in. This was the first time I addressed the media in person.

A reporter asked, "Governor, did you speak with the victims?"

"I did. Their stories are moving. Thank God they're here, but we have a lot of people who aren't."

That was tough to say out loud, but I knew I had to address the reality of the situation and recognize the massive loss of life we were facing. I explained the steps we had taken and the emergency orders I had given, and I let the reporters know we were working to save as many lives as possible. I also felt compelled to address the larger situation, saying, "We're not going to give in to terrorism."

I finished up by talking about fellow New Yorkers, the victims, and their families, who had been profoundly affected this terrible morning: "We're going to do what we can to help the families who lost loved ones, and we are going to protect and rebuild this city."

We left, got back in the SUV, and made our way farther downtown. As we drove south, heading directly toward the site, everyone in the car was silent. We looked ahead, gazing at the smoke still rising. The wind was blowing, pushing the tall stacks of smoke out of the way. It gave us the clearest picture yet of the devastation. The skyline of Manhattan had been changed forever.

We slowly pulled up to the area that would eventually be known as Ground Zero. The mix of emotions that hit me was overwhelming. Anger. *How could someone do this?* Sadness. *All of the lives lost.* Concern. *Will there be more attacks?* Determination.

We got out.

The scene was apocalyptic. You could see the air. You could taste the air. Just breathing left the taste of charred metal, ash, and death in your mouth. It was surreal. Shredded paper was pouring out of the sky. In some sick, twisted way, it looked like one of the ticker-tape parades for the Yankees on Wall Street after they'd won the World Series, with confetti raining down from every direction.

In that moment, there at the site of the fallen towers, I made it a point to not stick my face in front of cameras or speak to any media. This was not the time or place. I had already done one on-camera interview that morning at the hospital, giving out critical information. Now, it was time to quietly meet with the first responders on the ground and make sure they had all they needed. I let them know I was there for them, no matter what. However, I had to be smart about this.

I met with the acting fire and police captains to assure them we were there to help. I had been reluctant to seek out the leaders of the New York Police Department (NYPD) and the New York Fire Department (NYFD) who were in charge at Ground Zero, for a few reasons. First, the dark reality was that many of them were dead. Gone. Top leaders who responded died when the towers fell. Second, I did not want to get in the way of the people who had just been thrust into leadership positions. They were doing everything they could to continue to save lives, put out fires, and keep the area safe. I gently made my way around talking to some of the first responders. They were getting aid or taking a quick breather or drink of water while working the massive scene.

After some time there, as I walked a few blocks north of the site, I noticed large groups of people gathering. They formed a line. I assumed they were waiting for some sort of transportation, to be taken away from the horror of Ground Zero. I shook some hands to reassure them and asked what they were waiting for.

New Yorkers are often described as hardened, sometimes careless. I beg to differ in a big way. That tragic morning, men and women who either had escaped or worked nearby lined up for blocks to donate blood. They stood resolute next to the site of one of the most violent attacks in our nation's history, a place where more terror attacks were a distinct possibility. They were there to give blood, hoping to save a life. I was in awe. I approached the massive crowd, shook hands with people, and said, "Together, we will get through this."

New York is full of resilient and caring people who have been put through extraordinary tests. On that dark morning, they shined.

The firefighters, police officers, emergency medical technicians, and others, including battle-tested veterans, would face the greatest challenge of their career that day—saving civilians, saving one another, and later, recovering. The first few hours after the terror attacks, firefighters and police offers were in too much shock and too busy to process what had happened. The days after 9/11, more than the horrendous historical day itself, would wear on them like nothing before. For weeks, they dug through massive piles of twisted steel, concrete, and smoldering fires, recovering the bodies—or, horrifically, parts of bodies—of innocent men and women, including their own friends and relatives and fallen fellow firefighters.

From Long Island, to Buffalo, to the North Country, everyone in the state would soon be tested. The attacks were one thing. The economic and emotional fallout would be another.

CHAPTER 4

THE CIRCULATION OF CONFIDENCE IS BETTER THAN THE CIRCULATION OF MONEY

THE ECONOMIC CHALLENGES OF 9/11 WERE IMMEDIATE; SO WAS the emotional toll.

Widows. Widowers. Grieving parents. Dead children. The numbers were staggering: 2,606 civilians, 343 firefighters, and 71 law enforcement officers died in the World Trade Center.

The funerals were endless. The memorials were uniquely sad because for so many families, there was no body to bury. This was the beginning of the grieving process, one so emotionally devastating, so inconceivable, that it seemed the profound sadness would never end.

I attended more funerals than I can remember, as did virtually every member of my administration as well as my wife, Libby. We went to almost three thousand funerals; we wanted the state represented at as many as possible.

I recall two in particular, for distinctly different reasons.

Moira Smith was the only female NYPD officer to perish in the attacks. She had been one of the first to respond at the towers and help with evacuations. Moira was described as being calm but fully in command while she helped lead countless survivors to safety.

Moira's funeral was held at Saint Patrick's Cathedral. A heart-breaking image I can still visualize is her little girl looking up at me. Her daughter, only two years old, stood there holding hands with her father, unaware she had lost her mother. It was so emotional because it was different. I went to plenty of funerals where the father had been killed. This was the only funeral I attended for a mother.

When I spoke at the funerals, I conveyed that we would never forget those who had lost their lives saving others. We should be proud of what they did and proud of who we are as a nation. We weren't attacked because of anything we did wrong. We were attacked because of what we do right. We believe in freedom—freedom of religion and freedom of speech. Although we have sacred documents like the Constitution that provide a framework for those freedoms and our belief system, ultimately, it's the people who uphold our laws, especially those on the front lines, who ensure that our freedom is real. Without heroes like Moira Smith, our freedoms don't exist.

Another funeral, this one for a Staten Island firefighter, sticks out among hundreds of others for a different reason: there were so few people there. Before September 11, when I had gone to a funeral like this, there were thousands of firefighters lined up out front for blocks with a full bagpipe band from the Emerald Society. At this funeral, there was only one man on the Great Highland bagpipe.

Large numbers of people simply weren't available to pay respects to this man for several reasons. So many firefighters died in the attacks, so they weren't there. The magnitude of loss was massive. At the same time, the threat of more terror attacks was high, so surviving firefighters and police officers had to remain on duty. They could be spread only so thin. Meanwhile, hundreds of firefighters remained at Ground Zero, digging through rubble—at first to save lives, and then searching for remains. New York couldn't muster the normally appropriate response to bury this hero—a hero who, like so many of his fallen brothers, had rushed into burning buildings to save lives.

So, this young man who had rushed into the World Trade Center was buried with only a handful of firefighters there along-side his family. The small showing was not a true reflection. There was an inability, not a lack of will, to have a major turnout for such a loss. This was profound. It compounded the magnitude of grief and loss our city faced.

For months, as first responders were laid to rest, bagpipe tributes started and ended newscasts around the nation. Among the dead, one particularly powerful and haunting picture often appeared in newspapers, and magazines, and on television. It was the body of the NYFD chaplain, Father Mychal Judge, being carried out of the North Tower by firefighters and a civilian.

After the first plane hit, Father Judge rushed to the scene. He immediately began praying over the dead who had already been brought out of the building. As he prayed, hundreds more firefight-ers rushed into the North Tower. Without hesitating, he followed them in, continuing to pray aloud. Inside, Father Judge settled in at the emergency command post set up in the building.

Then the second plane struck the South Tower.

Standing one thousand feet below two infernos of hell that burned in the towers above, Father Judge continued his prayers out loud. More first responders rushed in. Hundreds of employees poured out of the buildings; they were the lucky ones.

At 9:59 a.m., the South Tower collapsed. An avalanche of debris came barreling down and then shot out in every direction. Aloud, Judge prayed, "Jesus, please end this right now! God, please end this!" Windows exploded with debris bursting through them, punc-turing parts of the North Tower.

Father Judge was hit. It was fatal. He was sixty-eight years old.

In life, as we age, we come to grips with our own mortality while attending funerals for those typically older than us who have passed away—a grandma, grandpa, mom, or dad. While the nation focused on that picture of Father Judge's lifeless body, September 2001 continued with endless, bodiless memorials of an entire generation of young firefighters, police officers, and Wall Street workers who had been wiped out. There were hundreds of funerals for men and women in their twenties and thirties. Among them were civilians just as heroic as the first responders.

One brave young man was an immigrant from China. Zhe "Zack" Zeng had come to the United States from Guangzhou, China, in 1988. Over the next ten years, he went on to graduate from the University of Rochester and land a job serving as an assistant treasurer at the Bank of New York on Barclay Street, just three blocks north of the World Trade Center. When the planes hit, his building was evacuated. Instead of fleeing for safety, Zeng, a volunteer certified emergency medical technician, grabbed first aid and medical supplies from his building and headed directly to the towers. Only minutes later, he was working side by side with firefighters to help the injured and guide them to safety. He died when the buildings collapsed. Zeng was twenty-nine years old.

Another selfless young man, twenty-four-year-old Welles Crowther, grew up in Nyack, New York, about an hour's drive north of the city along the Hudson River. Every Sunday, young Welles watched his father get dressed for church. His dad would always wrap a small comb in a red bandana, which he kept in his pocket. His dad passed along that red bandana to Welles. It became his trademark. He carried it everywhere with him, even wearing it under his high school sports uniforms. As a teenager, Crowther followed in his father's footsteps and became a volunteer firefighter. A scholar and an athlete, he went to Boston College, where he played lacrosse. When he graduated, he moved to New York City and took a job as an equity trader. That job landed him on the 104th floor of the World Trade Center's South Tower.

At 8:46 on the morning of September 11, the first plane hit the North Tower. Minutes later, the second plane hit. Crowther called home and left a message: "Mom, this is Welles. I wanted you to know that I'm okay." After that, his actions saved countless lives.

The second plane hit the South Tower between floors seventy-seven and eighty-five. Crowther headed down flights of steps directly into the inferno, entering the seventy-eighth floor's sky lobby. There, he ran into a group of survivors. With fires raging and smoke pouring through the windows, floors, and walls, Crowther put his red bandana around his nose and mouth and began directing people to safety, administering first aid and helping put out fires. Crowther, now known as "the man in the red bandana," carried an injured woman down seventeen floors only to turn around and head right back up the steps. He returned to the sky lobby and helped save even more people.

It wasn't until March 2002 that Crowther's body was found. The civilian, a hero, was lying alongside several firefighters in what was believed to be a command post in the South Tower lobby.

Zack Zeng has a city street dedicated to him, and Crowther's heroism lives on in stories, TV shows, and a documentary aptly titled *Man in Red Bandana*. These are only two of hundreds of stories about people of all ages, from all walks of life, who sacrificed their lives saving others.

The survivors, countless young people from all over the country, attracted to the action, culture, and energy of the city, along with mothers, fathers, and others who had made New York their home, wondered, "Will I ever work in or even go to the city again?"

Some businesses lost hundreds of employees in the attacks. Cantor Fitzgerald, a financial services firm that occupied the top five floors of the North Tower, lost a staggering 658 people.

Ground Zero was many things at that time. It was a nightmarish, apocalyptic scene, full of fires, smoke, and massive piles of debris. It was a rescue scene, where people worked around the clock trying to reach survivors. It was also a sacred place, where victims' bodies were being recovered. Finally, Ground Zero was an active crime scene, where thousands of people had been murdered.

Owners and members of corporate boards of nearby businesses began looking out their windows—literally looking down at the ashes of what had once been the pillars of the Financial District. Many others had no office at all. More than ten million square feet of office space had been destroyed. Millions more were damaged beyond repair. There was no electricity and no water to be found in the area. Soon, some businesses began relocating to temporary offices in Midtown. Others sent their employees out of state entirely to cities like Boston and Philadelphia. They paid for travel, hotels, and new housing. They wanted their employees to feel safe and secure, attempting to restore some semblance of normalcy to their lives and their companies. The situation was grim. The city was on lockdown, and the National Guard was omnipresent. While dealing with personal and security issues and the ongoing threats of other attacks, New York also faced an immediate economic crisis.

* * *

THAT FRIDAY, ONLY DAYS AFTER THE ATTACKS, AS I WAS IN MY Manhattan office, a call came in.

"Governor, I have a problem." (During this time, most calls began this way.)

It was Kenneth Chenault, the head of American Express, a pillar among financial institutions in the world and one of America's great companies. Amex was anchored right in downtown, directly across the street from the massive piles of rubble where the World Trade Towers had once stood. Ken had been with the company for decades and had landed the job of CEO that year.

"Governor, I have a board meeting on Monday. They're going to vote to recommend we leave the city."

Not good.

This was disappointing, to say the least, but after all I had been going through, I was focused and ready to take on any problem and find a solution. This one would be tough.

"Governor, I don't want to leave Manhattan, but the board is recommending we do so"—he paused and finished with two words: "right away."

As I began to take a breath to speak next, he launched into what his employees and the company's leadership had witnessed only days ago. His words became slightly more intense and urgent.

"We are right across the street. What we saw...." He paused; he was reliving it. "We saw the attacks happen, and Governor, this isn't the first time. A lot of our employees saw the same thing when the towers were bombed in '93."

His business, along with countless others in the densely packed downtown, had been through tough times before. Now, though, a visual hell on earth was next door and still smoldering before their very eyes.

"Governor, I do *not* want to abandon Lower Manhattan and send a message that the terrorists won. I want to stay. I want to encourage my board to stay, and I want to remain right here, across the street from where the towers stood."

The economic cost of losing Amex would have been terrible. But the symbolic loss would have been far worse. If Amex left, it would have sent a message to the world: Manhattan is no longer safe. It would have also triggered a domino effect. If Amex left, countless other corporations would have also felt immediately free to relocate. An Amex departure would have opened up the floodgates for a flight from downtown, and the final destination would not necessarily be another part of the city or state. They could have left New York entirely, possibly lured by tax incentives in Connecticut, New Jersey, or Massachusetts, where many companies had temporarily relocated to secondary offices anyway. Or they could head south to Texas or Florida, places with no income tax whatsoever. I was determined to keep Amex downtown, as well as every other business thinking about leaving. This would take some creative thinking, hard work, and immediate action.

CHAPTER 4

* * *

BEFORE 9/11, I HAD A CLEAR AGENDA. I WAS FOCUSED ON STRENGTH-ening New York's once dire financial conditions and ending our status as the most dangerous state in America. We worked tirelessly to reduce taxes, create a booming economy, and develop a healthier social climate.

The day the terrorists attacked our city, my focus on big-picture projects, positive projections, and plans all came crashing down. Immediately after devoting our resources to the health, safety, and welfare of the city and state, I had to turn to a basic goal—*keeping people in the city.*

As I traveled all over Manhattan and the other boroughs, meeting with people and taking calls, I would gaze out the car window and watch smoke billow from the site every minute of every day. I'd look down the streets. Eerily, they were empty. You could look ahead, spotting every traffic signal for miles, block after block. I'd listen. No horns. No buzzing cars. No jackhammers. No hum from crowded sidewalks that were normally filled with people heading to work or tourists snapping pictures. The city was empty and almost dead silent.

When night rolled around, closer to the debris you could see the site still lit up with a glow from fires that continued to burn. It was surreal and nightmarish.

With that visual in mind, as I took meetings and calls, I had to keep asking myself, "What can we do to stop people from fleeing the city and the state?" It was tough, but I needed to empathize with the heads of these companies and understand what they and their employees had been through. Regardless of their high stature and powerful positions, they were people too. All of us had been shaken. These men and women were dealing with a massive loss of life in their companies, the loss of family and friends. They had witnessed a scene that was nothing short of the worst horror film you've ever watched. Many of these businesses, like American Express, were located right next to what was now a massive homicide scene—*a homicide scene.*

This was a dark time, reflected in my calls, meetings, and conversations with colleagues in government, community leaders, and prominent heads of companies. It was one thing to hear from struggling CEOs and hedge fund managers; it was entirely different to visit a theater on Broadway and meet the thousands of stagehands, actors, and restaurant and service workers who were about to be laid off or had already been let go.

A sad and symbolic example of how job loss rippled throughout the city was represented in the empty, desolate Theater District. The streets, which night after night had always been full of excitement and energy, were now bleak and lifeless. The theaters went dark. No one could be seen for blocks. Hotels were empty, their lobby bars and restaurants lifeless. The shock of job loss was initially felt downtown. Now, other parts of the city were feeling the impact. More dominoes tumbled.

Without theatergoers, there's no Broadway. With no Broadway, there are no theater actors. Without actors to see, there are no people coming to stay at the hotels. With no foot traffic in the areas, there are no restaurants. Without the restaurants, there are no jobs for the managers, dishwashers, and servers.

The infinite chain of workers and artists who lost their jobs demonstrated the intertwined economy of Manhattan. It also exemplified the massive challenges ahead. Some New Yorkers ran out of money for rent. Others struggled to put food on their family's table. Thousands of people were being laid off at a time. It was spinning out of control.

We needed to figure out how to keep people living and working in the city, knowing also that doing so would help us with yet another huge challenge—tourism. The tourism industry is a major component of the state's economy; it's part of what keeps the city churning day after day. We needed to lure people in from around the country and the world. If we didn't do something radical, we would lose locals and the tourism industry altogether. Manhattan could have easily fallen back into the state of desolation of the 1980s and early '90s, with crime running rampant.

As we dealt with the immediate economic effects of 9/11, we were also still picking up the pieces in the aftermath of the dot-com bubble that had not just burst but *exploded*, leaving behind bankruptcies and job losses.

That September, our state still didn't have a budget set, and we tried to get it done by April. We were late. I personally rejected the legislature's budgets through vetoes. It was a classic Democrat-versus-Republican scenario. The Democrats wanted to raise taxes and spend more, relying on Wall Street revenue that simply didn't exist. I wanted to cut taxes, spend less, and grow the economy. We would end up having this fight for twelve years, and still, every year our state cut taxes, something I am proud of today.

From the late '90s into 2000, the market had had a period of insane speculation. Many dot-com companies had boomed; many had failed. Shortly before 9/11, the market had been in a tailspin because of the dot-com crash. I had foreseen that revenues would fall, and I believed the country was heading toward a recession. With a hunch that the dot-com fallout would be bad, I knew the state had to adjust accordingly.

It was actually a talking sock that convinced me the economy might be, *could be*, a bit unrealistic. Yes, a talking sock.

Do you remember Pets.com? It was a company that became a giant symbol of the tech bubble bursting. The company lost nearly $150 million in less than a year. It burned through cash while propping up a high-profile talking dog sock-puppet that cracked jokes on TV and marched in the Macy's Thanksgiving Day Parade. By the time the dog sock-puppet was getting interviewed on *Good Morning America*, I figured a crisis was around the corner. The sock puppet wasn't selling pet products, nor was it garnering much confidence for the company's ridiculously overpriced stock.

With no sock puppet on my hand or any other gimmick to entice businesses to stay, I continued to struggle with how to lure people to New York and keep them there.

I knew this: it had to start with everyone's coming together to reclaim a sense of optimism. And only in America, *only in America*, can you find the kind of optimism displayed by all New Yorkers and the country alike after the attacks.

We refused to let the pessimism take over. I refused to allow the city or state to fall into desperation. Tourists weren't coming because they thought New York was simply too dangerous. We had to fight back, and that would require what some political pundits and consultants call "optics."

Fighting back meant we needed an all-out blitz of positive messaging in the media. It meant that I, along with supportive surrogates, would have to be as present as possible in local, national, and international news, spreading the word that New York was bouncing back. Rudy Giuliani and I took to the air, running ads touting the idea that New York was still a great place to visit.

Along with optics, our recovery required bold leadership, demanding unique legislation from the city and state. This meant Democrats and Republicans had to work together. It would also require some convincing and negotiating with companies such as American Express and countless others. I knew these companies had to stay for so many more reasons than contributing to our tax base or any other impersonal business statistics. We needed them to stay for both tangible *and* symbolic purposes. It was part of what would boost confidence and optimism among downtrodden New Yorkers.

Amex would be first.

My call with CEO Ken Chenault continued. He went from slightly frantic to firm: "Governor, we need guarantees. I want to stay, but I need assurances. We're American Express. There's no more symbolic company in the world to the terrorists than American Express. We're asking for your help to assist in providing special security and special arrangements to protect us."

He told me that he had spoken with city officials who could not guarantee him anything special or out of the ordinary. But when he called me, I knew I could and would make things happen.

"Ken, we'll do it. The state will help. I personally guarantee you will have whatever extra security or security measures American Express needs to stay. It will happen."

He replied, "Okay, Governor, let me see what I can do."

That was it.

On Monday, while Ground Zero was still burning, he went in and convinced the Amex board to vote *not* to leave Manhattan. The board came together and, almost incredibly, agreed to stay another ten years.

I cannot stress how important this was. If American Express had announced it was leaving Lower Manhattan because of the attacks, it would have sent a clear message to the world: *Manhattan is dead; get out now*. Other companies would have fled and done so with the blanket of immunity provided by corporate giant Amex saying it was okay to leave.

Ken Chenault is a hero and a patriot. We didn't have a written agreement, not even a handshake. We had only talked by phone. Without this man's determination and leadership, the terrorists would have won an immediate symbolic battle. Lower Manhattan might be a ghost town today.

I called a special session of the legislature days after the attack, and lawmakers came to Albany—not as Democrats or Republicans but as New Yorkers. We worked day and night to address everything. The state stepped in and provided security not only to Amex but to other businesses downtown. I took things a step further, knowing we needed to do something to both keep businesses downtown and spur growth. I went with what I knew would help, offering a massive package of incentives, hoping businesses would respond. Assistance also came from Washington, where I spent weeks meeting with everyone from the president to House and Senate leaders.

We ultimately succeeded in receiving twenty billion dollars in federal aid to help us rebuild Lower Manhattan.

My plan, which was eventually adopted, created state- and federally-funded benefit packages for businesses, using concentric circles, with the smallest circle closest to Ground Zero receiving the greatest benefits. From there, we expanded circle after circle, with slightly fewer benefits in each one that was farther out. The circles stretched all the way to and around Chinatown. This plan and the offers in it, thankfully, began working unbelievably well. Business owners responded. By the day, more and more expressed interest, signed up, and let us know they would stay in the city for the long haul.

The idea behind this was more than handing out tax breaks or incentives here and there. What I aimed to do was give New Yorkers a sense of community through working together. Those facing tough times would all be part of something bigger. Together, they would be part of a movement to stay in Lower Manhattan. They would become a community, sharing the goal of recovery and a common future.

With security guarantees intact, our economic plan working, and companies like American Express deciding to stay, we scored victories for employees, their families, and all New Yorkers. Small wins began pouring in for our hard-hit city.

More than that, it was all a massive symbolic win for the state. This symbolism became critical in the weeks after 9/11.

With Amex staying put, it was time for a shopping spree. We needed the country to see that New York City was safe. To help, I was ready to pull out my credit cards and cash. It was time to show fellow New Yorkers and the world that Manhattan was open for business. As I made plans with staff and security personnel to head out on a shopping trip, we knew we needed someone symbolic to come along. We needed someone quintessentially New York.

I didn't lose a relative or close friend when the towers fell, but after the attacks, whatever I had done, whatever I was striving for, had no meaning; it all just stopped. I think 9/11 affected every New Yorker dramatically in some way. A disaster brings out the best in people. I think about all those firefighters, policeman and citizens who responded. Many of them died heroically. It was human nature to respond, to want to drop what you were doing and help.

—Robert De Niro in *The Guardian*, September 13, 2011

Robert De Niro *is* New York, and New York needed him.

A couple of months after the attacks, the traffic was flowing and goods were moving, but the economy was still sluggish. To shake things up, Robert De Niro and I went on a shopping spree together. I'm not one to get starstruck, but this was a monumentally positive moment in time. My suits were outdated and inexpensive; his were beautiful, although not as flashy as in *Casino*. But neither of us needed suits or clothes or anything at all. We simply wanted to make a statement, and that we did.

With the cameras and reporters in tow, we went shopping downtown. De Niro bought a few suits. So did I. He snagged a few shirts. So did I. We grabbed a bite to eat. Pizza, of course! (*C'mon. You kidding me?*) The press coverage was great. Our shopping spree was a success! People around the country saw us and thought, "If they feel safe walking the streets, so can I."

But going out wasn't always easy.

In the weeks after 9/11, I made an effort to go out to dinner every night in the city. For symbolic, economic, and emotional reasons, I was determined to physically be next to and share meals with my fellow New Yorkers. I've never been one to crave a crowd's attention, but it was flattering and emotional to walk into some restaurants and receive words of support and sometimes applause.

On the evening of September 14, some of my staff and I were dining at a restaurant near our office when Danny, my head of security, walked briskly over to our table. He whispered to me just loud enough so the others at the table could hear: "Governor, there is a suspected explosive device at the Empire State Building. NYPD shut down all surrounding streets. We need to evacuate you immediately."

Midbite, I paused and looked around the dimly lit restaurant. Just a few other people were there. Like so many other restaurants after 9/11, it was almost empty. Candles cast a light on something I had not seen in a while—smiles. The few people who were there were eating, drinking, and celebrating life—their own life as well as the lives of others who had recently passed. I swallowed my bite, set my silverware down, and took a deep breath.

Now, you might recall, on the morning of 9/11, for the first time ever, I refused my staff and security's advice. Then, I did it again only a half hour later by refusing to leave my office; they had wanted me to evacuate because it was located near the UN. Well, by now, refusing was tradition.

I let out my breath, looked up at Danny, and in a soft but firm voice said, "No. I'm sorry, but I'm not leaving."

Danny didn't speak. He just looked me in the eyes and nodded. Again, he didn't need to say a word. In that look, before he turned to walk away, he conveyed to me, "Okay. I get it."

After dinner, we would go back to my office and work well into the night, formulating more plans, making more decisions, and drafting more emergency orders, all to keep the recovery effort moving forward. We needed to keep sending a clear and confident message that New York was recovering.

Amex's staying downtown was big. De Niro's shopping near Ground Zero was great. But one of the most prolific moments showcasing our country's resilience and pride came on October 30, 2001. The Yankees returned to New York to play game three of the World Series, the first in the series played at home. This was the first time since 9/11 that more than fifty thousand people came together in one place.

"For tonight's ceremonial first pitch, please welcome the President of the United States."

Sitting in Yankee Stadium, surrounded by patriotic fellow New Yorkers, I barely heard those last few words from the announcer. The crowd roared louder than I had heard at any sports stadium, ever.

The president's security team had warned him not to go. He went. While he was defiant, he had to take some precautions. He had to wear a bulletproof vest. That made throwing a ball much more difficult. I watched him warm up, but he was forced to do so under the stands. Not the best place to get your arm ready.

With all the challenges he faced, Bush knew he had to get the pitch right. He was admittedly nervous. He had to throw it hard and get it over the plate. Yankee legend Derek Jeter didn't make things any easier. Just before Bush walked out onto the field, Jeter said with a laugh, "Don't bounce it. They'll boo ya!"

Bush strolled onto the field, calm and confident. The crowd roared even louder. It was an amazing rush of emotion.

Bush walked onto the mound. He wasted no time whatsoever. He wound up, threw the pitch, and absolutely nailed it. A strike. And with some zip!

He walked off the mound as cool as he had walked onto it. He waved to the crowd, which got even louder, now chanting, "USA! USA!"

This pitch, *this game*, was about more than baseball. This was a rally. It was a rally for New York.

Images are more powerful than words. These types of moments—symbolic moments—were seared into people's minds, from Amex's staying put, to my shopping with Bobby De Niro, to Bush's throwing out the first pitch at Yankee Stadium. These were turning points that signified life would go on. These visual moments helped reclaim a sense of normalcy and optimism that had disappeared in New York when those towers came down.

Not everything was normal, though.

Normal had been thrown out the window the day of the attacks. From mundane things like traffic to the most basic economic challenges, returning to normal would take years. The political arena was no exception.

CHAPTER 5

THE ONLY LEGITIMATE RIGHT TO GOVERN IS AN EXPRESS GRANT OF POWER FROM THE GOVERNED

New York City
September 24, 2001

"WE SHARE THE SAME INDIGNATION TO TERRORISM. WE JAPANESE fight terrorism together with the United States of America."

Japanese prime minister Junichiro Koizumi, along with myself and Mayor Giuliani, finished our press conference at Pier 92 in the city. Rudy and I had welcomed countless foreign heads of state who visited New York after the attacks, offering their condolences and assistance. Just as we began to leave, Rudy asked, "George, could we have a private meeting?"

"Of course."

Rudy and I worked incredibly well together during 9/11, communicating better than ever. Heck, at times we were like an old married couple, knowing exactly what the other person wanted before we finished our sentences. We also clearly knew and understood our separate and distinct leadership roles as well as how to blend them. In passing conversations, I would say to friends, "I have Rudy's back, and he has mine."

We walked into a small room to talk. As we did, I felt an uneasy tension, something different from the anxiety right after the attacks. We went through the usual formalities: "How're you holding up? How are things?"

Then he dropped a bomb; I couldn't believe my ears: "Governor, you have extraordinary powers to extend my term in office."

My heart sank. Then came shock. *No!* I angrily yelled in my head in disbelief, but I kept a straight face and said nothing. I should have known, though. Rudy's term was up. He wanted to stay.

In the weeks after 9/11, I supported repealing term limits so Rudy could run for office again. At first, state Republicans and some unlikely allies also thought it might be a sensible move. But as time passed, it felt like a bad idea both as a matter of principle and politically. Soon, the idea of another term was getting shot down in the press, by the public, and by lawmakers on both sides of the aisle, even if it was for "America's Mayor."

New Yorkers were still trying to make sense of what had happened. We were doing what we could to return to some sense of normalcy, even if we occasionally considered some things that were usually out of bounds. But no one would come around to the idea of abandoning our core beliefs in democracy. Rudy, understandably, wanted to stay. I wanted him to stay as well, but not at the expense of our democracy.

Let me also clue you in as to how politics and politicians work. Rudy's team was running an off-the-radar public relations campaign to extend his term in any way they could. While it may seem counterintuitive to leak information to the press, especially from a Republican camp, Rudy's team did so in order to influence the public and elected officials. They actively and aggressively leaked information, made requests, and had behind-the-scenes political and legal conversations with the media. But the backdoor attempts to influence lawmakers through the media weren't working. He had run out of options and came to me.

A repeal of term limits was off the table, yet here he was, asking for something more extraordinary: he suggested I cancel the election.

Cancel. The. Election.

My mind raced.

Are you really, right now, after a terror attack on our state, our city, asking me to just cancel the entire election? I am a conservative. We respect the law. For God's sake, you're a prosecutor! You know the law.

I said none of that aloud; I kept quiet and listened.

"Governor, you have the power to change the city charter to allow for me, as mayor in this time of crisis, to have an extended term."

He was partially right. I had already canceled and rescheduled the primary election, which, of all dates, was supposed to be on September 11. More than likely, Rudy thought if I had gone that far, I would also consider canceling the upcoming election and extending his term indefinitely.

Then and there, I knew what my answer was: *no*. For me, there was a huge difference between delaying a primary and suspending the election itself.

"I don't think I can do that, Rudy. It's not a good idea for you or the city, and I think it's beyond even my emergency legal authority to do this."

As if he knew I'd be skeptical, he excitedly fired back, "We've looked into it, and Denny thinks you do have the ability."

Denny Young was his counsel, who was in the room with us. So was mine, Jim McGuire. These two advised us on all legal issues affecting the city and state.

"George, can we have Denny and McGuire look into it?"

"Sure, but again, I really don't think it's legal or the right thing to do."

We left it at that and went back to work.

Rudy wasn't asking for martial law, but he was requesting that I take advantage of the tremendous and extraordinary powers extended to me as governor in a time of crisis. Undoubtedly, this was a time of crisis.

For weeks, Rudy's team pushed the issue with my staff. My team made it clear this was not going to happen. As it became clearer, Rudy asked for a brief meeting.

"George, you are right. I don't think you should cancel the election."

And with that, the matter was dropped.

Although Rudy's request disappointed me, maybe I shouldn't have been so emotional about it. While some may look at Rudy Giuliani as a power-hungry politician, the reality is that he wanted to keep leading and helping with the recovery efforts. He believed staying in office was best for the city. I was sure it wasn't.

The moniker "America's Mayor" was something Rudy Giuliani earned. Leaders are not born; they are made, often under the most difficult circumstances. This is something I learned about myself through the years. Mayor Giuliani was a true leader and displayed extraordinary leadership qualities on 9/11 and in the months after.

We all have our faults and temptations. Regardless of Rudy's motivation, regardless of his raw emotions in the situation, he abandoned some of the most basic conservative principles—follow the law and relinquish power when your term is over, even in times of crisis.

A peaceful transition of power would happen—no canceled elections, no term extensions.

I, Michael R. Bloomberg, do solemnly swear...
—upon assuming the office of mayor of New York City, January 1, 2002

Even if you've never been to New York City, I want you to visualize yet another symbolic moment.

There I was at Michael Bloomberg's swearing-in, on the veranda of city hall. I was watching the ceremony with hundreds of other city, state, and federal officials. We were several blocks north of

Ground Zero. It was January 1, 2002. City hall was behind us. The veranda faced south, looking out at where the towers once stood.

January.

This was almost four months after the attack.

As I watched Bloomberg take the oath of office, smoke rose into the sky behind the crowd. Plumes still billowed from the fire and wreckage of the World Trade Center towers.

January. Four months after the attack. Ground Zero was still burning.

It was surreal, but at the same time, as painful as the visual reminder was, that day was a testament to the resiliency of New York City and America. The image itself of the swearing-in ceremony, with smoke still rising over Ground Zero, spoke volumes. Only months after the worst terror attack our nation had ever witnessed, we stood strong as New Yorkers and Americans, calmly and peacefully witnessing the transition of power.

Government went on. Life went on.

In the months after 9/11, an amazing sense of patriotism abounded. We didn't go after people based on party lines or attack one another for being on one side or the other. The common thread of being American tied us together. It was truly a beautiful moment in American history.

In this crisis, like so many before during my time as governor, I learned lessons. At seventy-four years old, I am still learning. Life is a learning process, and when you are open to it, you learn to become a better, stronger person and a more effective leader.

In the political arena now, I'm not sure many people are open to learning or open to much at all, especially if something challenges their belief system. With the division, partisanship, grandstanding, and political calculating, we face a crisis of leadership. It's happening right now, and it is costing the American people dearly.

While some leaders throughout history have often found ways to create divisions, the most successful have inspired and unified. Nowadays, leaders divide.

CHAPTER 6

A HOUSE DIVIDED AGAINST ITSELF CANNOT STAND

God bless America, land that I love
Stand beside her, and guide her
Through the night with the light from above.

—"God Bless America"

Late afternoon in Washington, DC
September 11, 2001

There was once a time when we were unified.

Hours after the attacks of 9/11, *that same day*, members of Congress stood on the steps of the Capitol, held hands, and sang "God Bless America" together. It wasn't planned. It was a spontaneous moment after a press conference that brought people to tears of joy.

That moment in time was beautiful. In those fleeting few minutes, all partisanship and politics disappeared. There, on the steps of the Capitol, nothing mattered except that we were all Americans, unified regardless of age, ethnicity, or background. We were all together, here for one another with a hug, a hand, and a song celebrating our country.

CHAPTER 6

* * *

"Karl, he needs to be here."

It was September 13. I was on the phone with Karl Rove. I was frustrated, and he could sense it.

"Governor, I know, and I agree. The Secret Service doesn't want him to go. They have some serious security issues they're contending with, but we're going to make it happen."

The president needed to get to New York. I knew it. Karl knew it. And President Bush knew it.

Earlier in this book, I wrote that through the many tragedies I faced as governor, I learned the importance of *presence*. This was imperative for President Bush. The press had already unfairly been critical of him for not returning to the White House immediately after the attacks. In fact, Rudy and I were the highest-ranking officials omnipresent in those hours after.

A plan came together. The White House announced that the president would head to the city.

Later that day, Bush held a press conference at the White House. Rudy and I joined him by phone. He addressed us from a speakerphone with the press in the room: "I wish I was visiting under better circumstances, but it will be a chance for the three of us to thank and hug and cry with the citizens of your good area."

* * *

The president marked the next day with an official resolution from the White House:

> *Now, therefore, I, George W. Bush, President of the United States of America, by virtue of the authority vested in me by the Constitution and laws of the United States, do hereby proclaim Friday, September 14, 2001, as a National Day of Prayer and Remembrance for the Victims of the Terrorist Attacks on September 11, 2001.*

That morning, the president addressed a crowd at the National Cathedral in DC with a grave speech:

We are here in the middle hour of our grief. So many have suffered so great a loss, and today we express our nation's sorrow. We come before God to pray for the missing and the dead, and for those who loved them. On Tuesday, our country was attacked with deliberate and massive cruelty. We have seen the images of fire and ashes and bent steel.

After the ceremony, he boarded Air Force One bound for New York. I watched the live coverage on the news from my Midtown office, which had become like a second home. The reporters and anchors on every station worked nonstop around the clock. There were no commercials. There were no breaks. There was a steady stream of reporting on what happened, where things stood, and what was going to happen next.

It had already been a long morning. As I watched, I thought about the day ahead. It would be monumental. Danny broke me out of my daydream-like state. "Sir, we're ready. Air Force One is set to land soon."

I looked at him and looked back at the reporter on TV at Ground Zero, exactly where we were headed. I nodded. "Okay, let's go."

I stood up and followed Danny, watching his head dart around in every direction, always looking after my safety.

As we walked out of my office, a new security team called MRT, the Mobile Response Team, joined us. An elite unit of the state police, these guys now went with us everywhere. They carried MP5 submachine guns and concealed Glock nine-millimeter handguns. This was my new reality. It further cemented how serious the situation was following 9/11 and how much had changed overnight.

Danny and I, along with the new team of heavily armed men following in a chase car, exited the Midtown office. As soon as I stepped out the door, the silence once again struck me. New York is usually always so busy and so loud that the jackhammers, cars, horns, and people all become white noise. It's what makes the city great—the bustle, the movement, the people working and living. The streets that day were virtually empty. If any people were walking around, they talked to no one, kept their head down, and walked at a slower-than-usual pace for New Yorkers, in a state of stunned confusion. The silence became like a weight around my neck. It was not peaceful or pleasant in any way. It was a reminder of the responsibility I carried; I had to keep moving forward doing everything I could to ensure that the city would rise again from the ashes of 9/11.

I looked up into the sky. It was cloudy and drizzling. Like the streets, the sky was empty. The only noises from above were the occasional whirring of helicopters patrolling the skies and the intense blast of a jet fighter ripping through the sky. The choppers and jets that broke the silence also broke the temporary illusion of peace, reminding everyone that Manhattan was essentially a war zone.

"Governor, let's go."

Danny, the heavily armed team, and I got into the SUVs and headed to the nearby heliport. There, we hopped in a helicopter and headed to New Jersey's McGuire Air Force Base. McGuire was the only place the Secret Service deemed safe enough to fly into. Rudy and his team would meet us there, where we would greet the president.

Every step of the way to New Jersey was an awful reminder of the situation. Every block had some presence of law enforcement or the National Guard. When we got into the helicopter and began to ascend, I gazed out the window staring at the massive columns of smoke still rising from Lower Manhattan. As they ascended, they dispersed and became dark clouds of death, full of the ashes of the victims, the terrorists, and burning remnants of the towers. You could see them for miles.

We landed at McGuire. Like Manhattan, the only sounds were the hums of nearby helicopters on patrol, the buzzing of jets, and the chatter among the hundreds of security members and government officials at the base. The amount of security people there left a lasting impression. I couldn't even begin to count how many men and women surrounded the area, many openly displaying large-caliber weapons. Others were low key, likely carrying concealed weapons.

The mayor showed up shortly after. I watched him get out of the car and looked him in the eyes. From about fifty yards away, I could see the wear of stress on his face and a look of determination in his eyes. His jaw was clenched, and his lips were pursed together tightly, as they had been ever since the attacks.

"Hey, Rudy," I said as I reached out to shake his hand.

"George," he said, his voice a touch raspy.

There wasn't much chitchat. We had been working closely together every day. We were both exhausted but still going, beat but not pausing for even a minute. Then, in the silent skies above, we heard a hum in the distance. We looked toward the horizon. Air Force One was heading toward us, escorted by military jets. The hum became a roar as the massive Boeing circled the base and then landed.

The steps rolled up to the plane and the president exited, but not with the usual fanfare or photo ops. Press was kept to a minimum. The mood was somber and tense. As I watched the president descend the steps, I reflected on my time and relationship with him, long before he was commander in chief.

In the late 1990s, I considered running for president. Eventually, I decided against it, still wanting to get much more done in New York. I never thought I was somehow a chosen one, like some candidates do. I just wanted to make sure that if a Republican were going to run, it would be someone who had a philosophy similar to mine, had a record showing they could get the job done, and just as important, was someone who could win. George W. Bush fit all those categories. We got along well, and I thought he was unquestionably capable.

Bush and I had met a number of times. We had both served as governors, and we also went to Yale at the same time. He was a year after me. We knew each other at Yale, but not well. As we attended events for sitting governors over the years or connected for various other personal or professional reasons, we made a connection and got along really well. I was one of the first people to encourage him to run for president, long before other Republican governors. One year, Libby and I attended a White House dinner hosted by President Bill Clinton. We sat with Bush. After we finished our meals and headed out to get our coats, I pulled him aside.

"George, you have a minute?"

"Anything for you, Patak."

"Patak." This was my nickname. He rarely, if ever, addressed me by my first name or the title "governor." The always affable "W" has nicknames for everyone.

I smiled and called him by his first name.

"George, you really should consider running for president. I think you'd be great. Probably the strongest Republican contender."

"You think so?"

"Absolutely. You have the experience in the public and private sector, a great record in Texas, and of course, you've got the name ID."

Having the name ID, meaning name identification, means a lot of people know who you are. As a Bush, he had one of the most prominent names in the country.

He seemed surprised by my suggestion. Perhaps he thought I was planning to run. But I knew my words had an effect.

When he launched, I supported him in every way I could—helping with organizing, fund-raising, and providing advice whenever he asked. Furthermore, when his Republican primary challenger, John McCain, began winning a few races, we headed that off with a sweeping win in the New York primary. It was a critical victory that helped shore up his nomination. Over the years and challenges, we grew close. A few years after becoming president, he called me about something far more personal.

"Patak," he blurted out as I picked up the phone.

"Hello, Mr. President." I couldn't help but smile; his enthusiasm was contagious.

"Patak, ya gotta help me here. Barbara wants to go to Columbia, but you and I know how great it'd be for her to go to our alma mater."

He was referring to one of his daughters, who would be graduating from high school. She was considering Columbia University, an Ivy League school in Manhattan.

Of course I knew Yale was a fantastic school; so was Columbia. I knew something else, though: George W. Bush wasn't very fond of New York City. He hated the traffic, the chaos, and the big, overbearing personalities, especially the Wall Street types who attended political fund-raisers. Bush is a Texan through and through. His idea of a great time is clearing underbrush. Liberal New York City was not his cup of tea. That would change soon, though.

"My dad went to Yale. I went to Yale. I'd love for her to go. Now, your daughter goes there, right?"

"She does. Emily is there now. If you'd like, I can connect them. Emily can show her around."

"I'd love that. Thanks, Patak!"

Barbara connected with Emily a few weeks later. Emily told me they hit it off and had a blast touring the beautiful campus. They went to a party her sorority threw, and I'm absolutely certain they drank only ginger ale the entire time. Sure enough, Barbara chose Yale. She even ended up joining the same sorority as Emily, and later, my daughter Allison did too.

These years of memories hit me as President Bush descended the steps of Air Force One at McGuire. It was emotional, but it gave me a sense of comfort. Rudy and I waited on the tarmac to greet him. He approached us, first locking eyes with me. With his hand extended, he said the name I had heard so many times before.

"Patak!" he shouted over Air Force One, which was still humming.

President Bush has a tremendous ability to maintain his down-to-earth, friendly persona while still conveying empathy and communicating confidence. He can be upbeat but understanding and connected. While the press often poked fun at his mannerisms and speeches, after the attacks, the president offered comfort and stability, which the country needed desperately.

"Mr. President," I greeted him.

"It sure is good to see you both."

He looked over at Mayor Giuliani. They knew each other but not that well. Regardless, the president disposed of formalities.

"Rudy, how you doing?"

"Doing well, Mr. President."

I put my hand on the president's shoulder. "Mr. President, thank you for coming. It is great to have you here with us. New York needs you now."

President Bush then did something rare. He extended his hand toward Rudy and placed it just above his neck and behind his ear, like a father would comfort his son. The brief but powerful moment was caught on camera.

"Rudy, Patak," he said in a firm voice with his hand still on Rudy, looking at both of us, "we're going to get through this. I'm here for you. As we head into New York, you just let me know anything at all you guys need, and we will get it done. Anything. I'm here for you. The country is here for you."

With the Secret Service so on edge, there was no more time for conversation. We boarded the president's helicopter, Marine One, and ascended. The decoy helicopters that always accompany Marine One surrounded us, as did the large, double-bladed CH-46 Sea Knight support helicopters. Military jets also flanked us. We headed north toward the city, where the president would get a first-hand look at Ground Zero.

We shot north through Jersey, and then there she was—the Statue of Liberty. She stood tall. She stood resilient. Behind her those clouds of death billowed high in the sky. We buzzed past her and approached Manhattan.

We flew around the columns of smoke, circling Ground Zero. Seeing the devastation from the air was entirely different than seeing it on the ground. Looking down, we saw enormous holes in the ground surrounded by towering piles of debris. Stacks of steel were piled high like someone had tossed them into a giant heap of trash.

The three of us were silent as we looked out the windows, our views occasionally obscured when the wind shifted the smoke toward us. All I could think about was the catastrophic loss of life. Thousands of mothers and fathers, brothers and sisters from around the world were wondering if their family members had survived. Others were coming to grips with the fact that their loved ones would never come home again.

Marine One then took a sharp turn and quickly descended onto the Wall Street helipad, the closest place for aircraft to land downtown.

The moment we got out of the helicopter, we were ushered into the motorcade.

The car took off, accelerating at a high speed. We shot up the FDR Highway. There wasn't a car in sight on the usually congested road. Normally, getting over to the World Trade Center was a straight trip of a few blocks, but for this trip, with all the safety and security concerns, we took a different route. We headed north on the FDR and then veered into the city, going through a few neighborhoods before heading south to downtown.

As we got off the FDR and moved onto more crowded city streets, hundreds and hundreds of people lining the sidewalks held up American flags and signs. Every block was covered with people chanting, "USA! USA!"

We entered Chinatown. It was an amazing sight. Hundreds of people stood outside their businesses to watch the president roll by. They clapped and cheered and waved American flags as we made our way to Ground Zero. They too shouted, "USA! USA!"

As we passed by the patriotic crowds, my focus shifted from the New Yorkers to President Bush as he gazed out the window. For the past several minutes he'd had an intense stare without speaking at all, but now I noticed he was ever so slightly smiling. He noticed me looking at him. He looked over, flashed a slightly larger smile, gave a quick nod of approval, and looked back out the window.

Earlier, I shared how President Bush had had a disdain for the city, its aggressive atmosphere and constant chaos. In this moment, all of that melted away and he began to see New York City for what it was—Americans, from all corners of the world, living together in tightly packed neighborhoods, sharing the American dream regardless of their race, culture, or religion.

Despite all of the city's usual chaos, traffic, congestion, and crowds, after 9/11 President Bush would see the incredible diversity of people coming together. He would witness inspirational acts of strength and resilience. Eventually, he would come to love the city and its amazing people.

We knew the gravity of what we were about to walk into downtown, yet we couldn't help but smile. We were moved by this moment in time, happy to be together, supported by people from all walks of life. It was beautiful.

Then, reality began to set in.

The crowds faded the closer we got to Ground Zero. There were no more flag-waving Americans, only law enforcement and heavily armed military personnel, some in armored vehicles waving us through. Our motorcade slowed. We were arriving. I could hear all of us take a deep breath and let it out before we got out of the car.

We opened the doors, stepped out, and walked toward an area where firefighters and police officers had gathered. Across the street, a massive American flag hung off the side of a damaged building. Some first responders extended their hands for formal greetings. Others kept repeating, "Thank you. Thank you for being here."

There were also some quick, subdued bursts of applause. But the scene was solemn. Farther away, in destroyed buildings and on top of piles of rubble, hundreds of construction workers, hardhats who had been at the site for days, shouted out things like, "Thank you, Mr. President!"

But the emotions and feelings quickly turned darker. As we continued walking, a construction worker in the distance screamed, "We need to get these guys, Mr. President! Someone needs to pay!"

No one was chastising the president; people were venting. I began to see the emotions of 9/11 shift from shock to sadness to anger. By this day, September 14, first responders and construction workers had been working at Ground Zero nonstop for days. No sleep. No rest. They were agitated. They were angry.

The three of us reached Ground Zero. Firefighters were still recovering bodies. Fires burned. A heavy, thick smoke still hung around, and with it the smell and taste of death. We shook hands. We thanked people. President Bush made his way toward a large group that had gathered nearby. A few of the firefighters had found a fire engine buried under the rubble. They cleared the top of it so it could serve as an improvised stage for the president.

On top of the fire truck and ready to help guide the president was retired firefighter Bob Beckwith. Beckwith extended his hand and helped Bush climb up. He handed the president a bullhorn to address the large crowd. Secret Service members, rightfully cautious, told Beckwith to get down and away from the president. But Bush wasn't having it. He slung his arm around him and insisted he stay. The president began speaking and consoling:

I want you all to know that America today is on bended knee, in prayer for the people whose lives were lost here, for the workers who work here, for the families who mourn. The nation stands with the good people of New York City and New Jersey and Connecticut as we mourn the loss of thousands of our citizens.

As he spoke, the raw emotion, now boiling, seeped up. A few rowdy firefighters in the crowd shouted at him, "We can't hear you!" Bush's reply defined the first term of his presidency.

"I can hear you! I can hear you! The rest of the world hears you! And the people, and the people who knocked these buildings down will hear all of us soon!"

The crowd roared! Bush improvised and nailed the moment. He tapped into the anger and frustration so many of us felt. The crowd began shouting, "USA! USA!" It was a profoundly emotional moment—filled with sadness, anger, and hope. Hope that a better day was on the horizon.

We wrapped up at Ground Zero and returned to the motorcade to head north to the Javits Center, Manhattan's largest convention center. It has four floors and a total space of 1.8 million square feet. We needed it all. The size of the Javits Center again shows the epic proportion of the lives touched by this tragedy.

Shortly after the attacks, I had ordered staff to set up a command center for families to go to that would serve as a central location for information, possible answers, and, most important, counseling. At first, we opened it up at the Sixty-Ninth Regiment Armory, a large historical building on Lexington Avenue between East Twenty-Fifth and Twenty-Sixth Streets in the Rose Hill neighborhood. An older building, built in 1906, it is massive even by New York City standards, housing a five-thousand-seat arena.

This order, this specific order I demanded from staff, was a direct result of my lessons in the TWA Flight 800 crash. After that plane went down, families from New York and all over the country descended on JFK airport, desperate to learn what had happened to their loved ones. When they arrived, they had no direction, no information, and no clue where to get help. They scattered all over looking for help, guidance, and support in one of the worst moments of their lives. I vowed then that something like that would never happen again. If we ever had another event with a major loss of life, we would immediately set up a staging area where relatives and friends could get the information, assistance, and emotional support they so desperately needed.

As big as it is, the armory unfortunately presented problems right way. Out of hundreds of emotional moments with family members terrified of what might have happened to their loved ones, one stands out—a middle-aged man, distraught, with tears running down his face, turned and yelled at me, "Governor, they're hiding the bodies." There were no bodies; they were either destroyed or trapped under tons of burning rubble. I just went up to him and without saying a word gave him a big hug, with tears running down my face as well. Instantly the anger vanished. He knew that pain we all felt—nothing was being hidden. We were all suffering together. So many people came that it became dangerously crowded and uncomfortable. Doctors and mental health professionals shared another, subtler problem with us: the building was too dark. As families flocked to get answers and sadly began coming to grips with the loss of loved ones, they were trapped in this dimly lit building that only exacerbated their depression. So, we moved the family center to an open, airy pier on the Hudson River. The families were later invited to meet the president at the massive Jacob K. Javits Convention Center when he arrived after the attack.

Back at Ground Zero with the president on September 14, Rudy and I got into the limousine to head to Javits. But before the president did, he—always good-natured and super friendly—waved in the fire commissioner, the police commissioner, and the emergency services director.

"Come on in, guys!"

They hopped into the limo with us. All mashed together, we headed north. With his big smile and invitation, the president had disarmed the guys and even slightly lightened the mood. This was good, especially for Fire Commissioner Thomas Von Essen, who was devastated. He had just lost hundreds of his fellow firefighters, who were like family. Tommy was in a lot of emotional pain at the time but still had his sense of humor. After the president lightened the mood, Tommy told us a hilarious but very personal story I won't repeat here. He had us laughing hard.

Our motorcade continued north, this time on the other side of the island, heading up the West Side Highway. With our laughter dying down, the limo got quiet. We gazed out the window, passing by huge crowds chanting and cheering. For days after

September 11, massive groups of people lined the streets, waving flags, holding signs, and cheering every fire truck, ambulance, and support vehicle headed to Ground Zero. It was enormously inspiring.

My attention turned to the president. He looked out the window intensely, as if he were observing each and every person on the street. Ever so slightly, he started to grin. I spoke up: "Mr. President, look at all these people cheering for you. They love you."

His grin got larger as he continued looking out the window. I paused, then cracked a joke: "Sir, this is Manhattan. Not one of them voted for you."

The president quickly turned to me with his eyes wide open in amazement. Then he burst out laughing. "Ha! Patak, you're probably right!"

We followed, laughing out loud.

Without missing a beat, Rudy chimed in, "Yeah, and I don't think more than five of them voted for you, George."

I laughed even harder, because what he said was hilarious and also very true.

It was a lighthearted moment before another solemn visit.

If the president, Rudy, and I thought Ground Zero had emotionally taken a toll, this was another level of profound emptiness. Here, parents desperately paced back and forth waiting for information on missing children. Spouses waited nervously for anything at all on husbands or wives. Aunts, uncles, and grandparents pressed anyone and everyone for something, *anything*. In a daze, many wandered around the massive building aimlessly, hanging on to the faintest amount of hope that they would learn that a loved one had been recovered or found at a nearby hospital. And everywhere they held pictures, large photographs and poster boards of their loved ones, hoping someone, anyone, could tell them what happened.

Rudy and I followed the president into the center. Many in the crowd snapped out of their daze and approached us. The three of us split up and began shaking hands and hugging people. It was indescribably heartbreaking.

As I spoke with people in the crowd, one family stood out because they were so full of confidence. The mother walked up to me holding up a picture of her daughter. She held it high and put it directly in front of me.

"This is our daughter, Kathy. Governor, we know she survived. We know she's safe. She worked as a Port Authority officer. She knew the buildings. No one knew those buildings like her. She would have known exactly where to find shelter and take cover when they came down."

I stared at the picture, knowing that more than likely this young woman had died. As I listened, my heart sank. I felt terrible. I felt so terribly *sad*, but I kept my composure. For a second, as I stared at that picture of this young woman who was probably dead, my mind wandered. For just a few brief seconds, I exited the moment. I stared at that picture and saw my own children, each and every one of their faces filling it. I thought about how lucky I was. My kids and my wife were alive. My family was at home waiting for me. I brought myself back into the moment and looked the mother directly in her eyes. Impossibly, they were filled with hope and desperation at the same time. It was as if her brain was telling her one thing and her heart another.

Then, I thought about the firefighters at Ground Zero working every minute of the day to find survivors buried in the rubble. I thought, *who am I to tell this mother she's wrong? Miracles do happen.* Somehow, I found it in me to be pessimistic and optimistic at the same time.

"Ma'am, firefighters are working around the clock to find and rescue survivors. If she's alive, they're going to find her."

That brave officer was Captain Kathy Mazza, the Port Authority's only female officer to perish in the attacks. Mazza had been leading people out of the North Tower as it began to collapse. When the upper floors started to crumble, Mazza reacted quickly. She drew her nine-millimeter sidearm and shot out the massive glass walls of the tower. Hundreds were able to escape because of her actions. She was a hero. So many were that day.

In the days after 9/11, families prayed. They hoped. They yearned. Americans wanted more. Some wanted answers. Others wanted blood. They wanted justice for the thousands of innocent men, women, and children who had perished in the attacks.

President Bush tapped into that anger with his now famous response: "I can hear you! I can hear you! The rest of the world hears you! And the people, and the people who knocked these buildings down will hear all of us soon!"

The moment was extraordinary. But Bush's statement carries serious consequences to this day. *In times of crisis, the reaction is often far worse than the event itself.*

September 11, 2001, was terrible. Decisions made after that day set up long-term disastrous foreign policy decisions with equally horrifying political consequences. In the weeks after September 11, President Bush was extraordinary. He gave an outstanding speech to a joint session of Congress, addressed foreign leaders, and did numerous public and private events to inspire the American people.

In terms of foreign policy, rightfully, the United States went into Afghanistan to rid the country of Al-Qaeda training camps and demolish the group's base of support. We also began the hunt for the mastermind of the attacks, Osama bin Laden. This was exactly the right thing to do. President Bush deserves credit for fulfilling his pledge to retaliate against those who attacked us. Our mistake, though, was to stick around for almost two decades, attempting to nation-build and create some semblance of a democracy in a country that has no embedded tradition of it.

Then we invaded Iraq, a country that seemed to pose no threat to us.

The Bush administration argued that the country had weapons of mass destruction (WMD) and was a danger to the world. Vice President Dick Cheney pushed dubious connections between Iraq and the September 11 attacks themselves. I have no doubt that President Bush, like the vast majority of people in both political parties at that time, believed this to be true. It was not.

We attacked Iraq in the name of freedom and security. We targeted, removed, and eventually hanged Saddam Hussein, accusing him of possessing weapons of mass destruction, which were never found. Furthermore, neither freedom nor security would flourish in Iraq or the region. The area only became more dangerous and unstable.

I will be blunt: *the war in Iraq, driven by Dick Cheney, is the worst foreign-policy decision in recent American history.*

I do not believe for a moment that George W. Bush lied or deliberately misled America about the reasons for the Iraq War. I know George. He is too honest and has too much integrity to lie about a decision he knew would cost American lives. The information presented to the president, referred to as a "slam dunk" by the director of the CIA and the vice president himself, was, I believe, skewed to create a forgone conclusion that Saddam Hussein posed a real threat to America. He did not. However, a president can be only as good as the intelligence he or she is provided. And it wasn't just President Bush who received this intelligence. Colin Powell, a man of impeccable integrity, Hillary Clinton, and many others accepted the danger Saddam Hussein posed as fact. To this day, it would not surprise me to learn that some in President Bush's circle of advisors deliberately misled him and the American public.

Although the responsibility ultimately rests on the president's shoulders, if you're going to go to war, you had better be right about why. The premise in this case was WMDs, *and they weren't there.* The rationale was simply not true. It was a huge blunder to go into Iraq, and that decision changed everything.

The political cost of distrust, anger, and resentment cannot be measured today. The war in Iraq destabilized an entire region and allowed terror to flourish. The loss of life continues year after year.

On September 11, 2001, America was the victim, attacked in a vicious manner, which generated enormous global support for our response while isolating the radical Islamists who had carried it out. Four years later, America was the imperialist invader of a foreign country under false pretenses. The mission to bring terrorists to justice changed dramatically. We would now bring democracy, American-style, to parts of the world that had never seen it before. This became neoconservative nation-building; short-term goals became long-term. We had a shaky list of allies and became trapped in an endless war with an incalculable human and economic cost.

Other modern administrations, including President Ronald Reagan's after the Marine barracks bombing in Beirut in 1983, knew better than to immerse our military in a never-ending war in the Middle East. His successor, George H. W. Bush, knew this, too. After liberating Kuwait from Saddam Hussein, he stopped short of capturing Baghdad and removing Hussein. He did what was necessary to prevent the unilateral destruction of a country but stopped short of creating chaos by removing the Iraqi regime. He took an approach that kept balance in a region where the slightest tip of a scale meant more battles in the already war-torn area.

But this time, the United States went all in, launching a full-scale invasion with the premise that Iraq harbored WMDs and the regime needed to be removed. As we invaded a country that had nothing to do with 9/11, the Iraq War became a flashpoint that eroded our sense of unity and commonality at home and destroyed the moral high ground that America once had abroad.

No one can fault the sacrifices our brave soldiers made to bring peace to Iraq and Afghanistan. I went to Iraq in 2004 and again in 2006. My son Teddy served as a platoon leader in Iraq's Anbar province in 2006. And in Afghanistan, my son Owen served as a Lieutenant in the 10th Mountain division. The efforts of the Americans there to bring a stable representative government were tremendous.

Unfortunately, there were two massive challenges for the US. The first stemmed from the strategic blunder to send the Iraqi Army and civilians home after what was declared a victory. Unemployed and restless, they soon became a core part of the opposition to the occupation.

The second was more systemic. Wishful thinkers in Washington thought that by holding elections, the country would somehow form a vibrant democracy. It did not form one. It still has not formed one. To have a democracy, a country needs a free press, an educated electorate, an independent judiciary to uphold the rule of the land, elected officials respectful of the law, and a military free of political allegiances. None of that existed in Iraq or Afghanistan. From our initial invasion and lack of planning to President Obama's terrible decision to completely withdraw, our idea of creating democracies simply wasn't going to work. We created a void later filled by extremists and terrorists, eventually including ISIS.

At home, our country—which on September 11 had been unified and had the support of the vast majority of the nations of the world—found itself bitterly divided and virtually isolated internationally. With a greatly diminished prestige today, the War on Terror continues in Afghanistan, Iraq, Syria, Yemen, Libya, Mali, Niger, Nigeria, Somalia, and likely other countries that we, the public, don't know about yet.

Ask yourself: *Have any of these regions in the Middle East or Africa become safer places? Has terrorism ceased in the Middle East, Europe, Asia, or the United States?* No. In fact, in the Middle East, terror attacks have increased tenfold since the United States went into Iraq.

Must we remain engaged? For our own protection, yes. Before September 11, Al-Qaeda was allowed a safe haven in which to recruit and train terrorists to attack us here, with horrible consequences. That cannot happen again. But as a country, we must develop a realistic practical foreign policy to deal with radical Islam. After World War II, the policy was to contain the grave Soviet threat during the Cold War. Today, we need to establish a similar policy that confronts Islamic extremism but rejects the need for long-term military engagement in the name of nation building.

The absence of a long-term vision after September 11 has left much of the Muslim world and the West at odds. Vice President Cheney and Secretary of Defense Donald Rumsfeld drove an aggressive foreign policy agenda and hijacked the Bush presidency. We face the consequences today. The War on Terror has no end, and this never-ending war has a direct effect on our attitude and psyche here at home.

In times of war, policy differences become treason.

* * *

CHENEY, WITH THE AID OF RUMSFELD, DROVE US INTO WAR WITH A reckless, aggressive foreign policy. That decision to invade Iraq began leading Americans into the great divide. And as we neared the presidential elections of 2004, campaign rhetoric and strategy further divided our country.

George W. Bush is a sincere, patriotic, and caring man, someone who was put into positions most people simply couldn't face. From the pressure of being president to the "fog of war," as he once called it, it all must have been so grueling. Having served three terms as governor of a large, powerful state, including through September 11 and the aftermath, I know just how many people, advisors, voices, and suggestions you get on a regular basis. Some are selfish, and others selfless. Some are passionate; others don't care. And a select few are totally trustworthy. Sorting it all out can be maddening and exhausting.

President Bush's father, a wonderful man, was defeated in his quest for a second term. Now his son was facing the same prospect.

While a well-intentioned elected official governs based on a sincere belief in doing what is right for the people, once that politician gets closer to an election, political advice can sometimes drown out sound policy choices. For Bush, that advice came from Karl Rove.

The tone took shape on the night of the president's State of the Union address in January 2004. I had high hopes for this speech. I wanted Bush to make a call for unity, build on themes that brought us together, and reflect on our commonalities as Americans. But the great divide had begun, and the Iraq War was at its epicenter.

Though the war and subsequent failures began to divide the country, the problem wasn't just foreign policy. It was the vitriol espoused by both sides leading up to the invasion and after it. The "you're either with us or against us" attitude, when it came to supporting or opposing the war in Iraq, pervaded both sides of the political spectrum. Bush's approval ratings, which had been sky high immediately after 9/11, were sinking dramatically and quickly. Antiwar protests were being launched across the country. In dramatic fashion, the protests got personal, nasty, and ugly in ways we've rarely seen in America. Extremists on the left began burning effigies of President Bush and slapping Hitler mustaches on pictures of him that they hoisted in front of the cameras for the nation and world to see.

This was the start of something new, something more extreme. These were personal, aggressive attacks portraying violence against President Bush. The extremists strung him up, hanged him, and burned him. With the mustaches, they compared him to a man who had put millions of Jews to death. It's one thing to criticize policy; it's another to demonize people who have a different political view. Other radical-left protestors burned the American flag, something that had been unimaginable only a few years before!

With lines being drawn between prowar and antiwar elements among both Democrats and Republicans, I desperately hoped the president would use this platform to unite and inspire. The love after that dark moment in our history was still there, even if only as a faint glow in Americans' hearts. Someone could reignite it, recapturing that sense of patriotism and unity we felt only a few years before. I hoped the president would do exactly that. He did not. Responding to the vicious attacks from the left, the Bush campaign developed a strategy that ultimately increased the great divide. That strategy was executed in Bush's 2004 State of the Union speech.

The night of the State of the Union speech, I made it a point to clear my schedule of calls or any other distractions so I could watch intently. Key staff members joined me at the governor's mansion in Albany to watch the president. It was shaping up to be a nice night. For political animals like us, the State of the Union is like a playoff game, but not quite a championship. That would be election night.

We had dinner together, shared some laughs and glasses of wine. Then it was time. We finished eating and headed into the TV room, which had couches and chairs spread out in front of a large-screen television.

"John," I said to my relatively new chief of staff, as he sat down next to me to watch this historic event.

"Governor."

John Cahill may have been raised in Yonkers, but the Bronx-born New Yorker still had his accent, hitting his consonants hard while slightly dropping his r's. I had appointed him to chief of staff only a couple of years before.

John is someone of impeccable integrity. A six-foot-two son of Irish immigrants, he participates in Ironman triathlons and still has the same slim, athletic build today as he did years ago. He also has piercing blue eyes, which, like his personality, are disarming and intense. The affable yet no-nonsense and to-the-point personality that John exudes every day has earned him respect from people in politics and in the private sector.

John was always more than a chief of staff to me; he was, and still is, a friend. He's also a fighter. As governor, there were so many issues I had to focus on that I could sometimes get stretched thin. John helped steer the ship, and when I needed to get a deal done or legislation passed, I trusted him completely. I felt about John the way I did about my entire team. They were family. You never want people working for you out of fear; you want a deep personal commitment.

We settled in the chairs and couches around the TV. The president was about to begin. As he started, we observed. And we waited. We waited for something with some substance.

As Bush's speech floated between Iraq and domestic policy, we watched, sometimes incredulously, sometimes in amazement. Some people in the room gave a "huh?" or an "ugh." The speech itself went from disconnected to downright bizarre.

Parts of the speech were clearly defensive. Bush was facing intense criticism for going to war without the support of traditionally allied countries. He cited some of the countries that had joined us, such as Great Britain and Australia. Later, he weirdly worked in a big thank-you to Thailand and El Salvador.

He was also defensive about the reason for going to war, namely weapons of mass destruction. In his speech, Bush stated, "Already, the Kay Report identified dozens of weapons of mass destruction-related program activities and significant amounts of equipment that Iraq concealed from the United Nations."

Less than a month later, the author of the Kay Report, David Kay, who was also the head of the Iraq Survey Group, known as the ISG, resigned. Kay stated that the ISG couldn't find any WMD stockpiles. He bluntly said, "I don't think they existed."

In this speech, at a time the American people needed someone to lay out a global vision filled with optimism and hope, Bush did not make a single call for unity. He used the word "together" exactly five times. They were calls to members of the House and Senate, asking them to work together on issues like taxes and health-care costs. He did not call for unity among the American people.

Then, Bush's State of the Union speech veered off into sex and steroids.

"What?!" you ask.

Yep. Sex and 'roids.

Now, as you read this, to make it even weirder, read it in his cadence and with that Texas twang perfected by *Saturday Night Live*'s Will Ferrell.

To help children make right choices, they need good examples. Athletics play such an important role in our society, but unfortunately, some in professional sports are not setting much of an example.

John Cahill, still seated next to me, became visibly uncomfortable. He was shifting in his seat repeatedly, leaning forward and gesturing toward the TV. He couldn't contain himself, blurting out, "What the hell is he talking about?"

Another staffer jokingly whisper-yelled, "Can someone pinch me? I want to know if I'm dreaming."

I couldn't stand it either. I was so upset and bothered by this speech, I stood up and began pacing as I watched it.

Bush continued.

The use of performance-enhancing drugs like steroids in baseball, football, and other sports is dangerous, and it sends the wrong message: that there are shortcuts to accomplishment and that performance is more important than character.

John unleashed again.

"This is unreal! We have a war going on. What is he talking about? Who fed him these lines? This is not him!"

Think about this time, place, and context.

It was only a few years after 9/11. The country had descended into anger and division with an ongoing war in Iraq no longer supported by half of Americans. Meantime, troops were still also in Afghanistan. Major allies like France and Germany weren't only openly questioning our foray into war, they were criticizing us. And here was George W. Bush, now a wartime president, delivering a State of the Union about athletes who hit little white balls with wooden bats. He was calling them out for being more concerned with "performance" than "character."

What...is...going...on?

Then, somehow, some way, things got weirder. Bush started talking about teenagers and STDs. Yes, you read that right—sexually transmitted diseases.

> *Each year, about three million teenagers contract sexually transmitted diseases that can harm them or kill them or prevent them from ever becoming parents.*

You know what this felt like? Think back to when you were young and happened to be watching some R-rated movie with your parents. Remember how incredibly awkward and uncomfortable it was to sit there with them when a sex scene came on? Yeah. That's exactly what it felt like watching "W" talk about teens and STDs.

Then, Bush talked about spending more taxpayer dollars. This, of course, after he had cut taxes, increased domestic spending, and had us deep in two wars.

> *We will double federal funding for abstinence programs so schools can teach this fact of life: abstinence for young people is the only certain way to avoid sexually transmitted diseases.*

That was it for John! He stood up and left, mumbling, "I can't take this anymore. I gotta go."

I wasn't even fazed by John's leaving. I didn't even say "bye." I continued pacing back and forth, without breaking my gaze at the TV. As Bush continued, I just shook my head, sighed, and whispered to myself, "Okay, Mr. President."

I went to bed not long after, asking myself, *was that as partisan and disconnected as I thought it was?*

The next morning, still in disbelief, I did something I rarely did as governor. I called the president. After letting the speech sink in for a night, I had grown more frustrated. I wanted him to invoke the spirit of September 11 and call for unity. I wanted him to address the growing divide between the American people and, at minimum, extend an olive branch and reclaim our common future.

The country needed inspiration from a wartime leader. There was none of it. It was the opposite of what I had hoped for and where I believed the country should be heading.

He answered.

"Mr. President," I said, in the polite way I usually greeted him. We made small talk until I got to the prior evening's speech.

"Mr. President, that seemed highly polarizing to me. Do you think that's the right approach as we head into a campaign year?"

His answer shocked me. "Yeah. Well, my team tells me Dean will get the Democratic nomination."

Bush's campaign team believed Howard Dean, the charismatic, provocative, far-left governor of Vermont would win his party's nomination and run against George W. Bush in the general election.

Then came the strategy. "Rove says with a candidate like Dean, we have to galvanize the people. We need to focus on motivating the base. We need to polarize. That will get me fifty-six to fifty-eight percent of the vote, which means a win."

Dean was such an inflammatory candidate that the Bush team felt provoked. They were convinced they needed to hit Dean hard while at the same time galvanizing and inspiring Republicans with specific issues. They were not interested in casting a wide net or winning over Democrats. This would be a base election, meaning they wanted to fire up Republican voters as much as possible and drive them to the polls.

In Bush's first election, Rove had felt disappointed by members of the evangelical base. They hadn't come out to vote in big numbers. That is precisely why the Bush team had included the ridiculous State of the Union themes about athletes, character, STDs, and abstinence. It was to appeal to fundamentalist Christians who didn't vote in 2000. They needed them in '04, so the campaign shifted away from unifying themes and instead worked to divide and conquer.

Ultimately, Howard Dean didn't get the Democratic nomination. It was someone else from Yale, who I knew fairly well: John

Kerry. He had been a year ahead of me and chairman of the Liberal Party student group on campus. I had been chairman of the Conservative Party student group.

In my experience, after you get the nomination, you reach out to as broad an electorate as possible, particularly the middle and moderate members of the other party. This polarizing strategy was new. This time the middle didn't matter. In fact, today it's a strategy both parties have widely adopted, with dreadful consequences—exacerbating our great divide.

This was a depressing phone call. We wrapped up. As I set the phone down, I felt a pit in my stomach. Bush had gone from his 2000 theme of being a "uniter" to being an unbridled divide-and-mobilize-the-base candidate.

I'm certain that the Bush campaign team believes that they ran the right campaign. Bush's father lost his reelection to Bill Clinton in part because the Republican base did not turn out as hoped. George W. Bush won his, barely squeaking by. Those elusive evangelicals who didn't appear in 2000 were absent again in 2004, despite the speech.

To this day, I believe that a race centered on uniting America in defense of our freedoms and finding common ground in the spirit of September 11 would have won him a resounding victory. Instead, he won with a very small margin of error. The Rove strategy, as disappointing as it was, worked.

* * *

LESS THAN A YEAR LATER, THE REPUBLICAN NATIONAL COMMITtee chose New York City as the location of its national convention, recognizing the center of those horrible September 11 attacks. As the governor of New York, as well as a friend and supporter of President Bush, I was invited to speak at the convention to nominate him for a second term.

As I prepared my speech, a famous phrase from President Abraham Lincoln echoed in my mind: "A house divided against itself cannot stand." Those words marked one of the darkest chapters of America history. They are still just as relevant. I knew what I wanted to accomplish. I wanted to bring people together. This was something I had done all my life, as a young man growing up in a poor and racially diverse area and as a political figure.

I've always believed that to be a successful leader, you must never stop fighting for the vision you hold, regardless of the challenges or setbacks in achieving that vision. Personally and professionally, I always tried to find ways to bridge divides. Politically, instead of simply winning with a narrow partisan ideology, I worked to govern in such a way that my core conservative philosophy supported me but allowed others to recognize our common future. Whether New Yorkers specifically, or Americans as a whole, we are in this together.

My focus on unity, my focus on a common destiny, my focus on all Americans led me to start my speech with a few stories that reached out to people from all over the United States, while touching the hearts of New Yorkers.

I started with an amazing and moving story from Oregon.

After September 11, our tourism industry was hit hard. Do you know what the people of Oregon did? A thousand people from Oregon came to New York and rented one thousand hotel rooms so our workers and desk clerks and waiters could keep their jobs. Where is the Oregon delegation? Oregon, please stand. Thank you.

I moved on to another heartwarming story from the Midwest.

After September 11, the people of Iowa heard that our guys at Ground Zero were getting cold working through the night. So Iowa rushed 1,500 quilts to help keep them warm. Iowa delegation will you please stand? Thank you.

I then reached out closer to home, to Pennsylvania.

Pennsylvania, where are you? Five brothers in your state had been saving for years to go to Disney World. They had saved almost $900. After September 11, the boys drove to Brooklyn to a firehouse that lost eight men. They gave their Disney World money to the relief fund. Pennsylvania, you raised those boys. Please stand. Thank you.

I paused and then shared local stories.

Now, I could tell a story like this about every single state in the country. But there was, of course, another state. It woke up one morning and walked the kids to school, and suddenly the streets were full of sirens and there was fire in the sky. You know what they did, the people of this state?

They charged into the towers. They stood in line like soldiers to give blood. And then, in the days and nights that followed, the tough men and women of our great city came forward. They quieted the fire and dug us out of grief. They got into trucks and went to Ground Zero, the construction workers and ironworkers, our police officers and firefighters.

And the people of our city stood in the dark each night, waving flags, and calling out "God bless you" as the trucks hurtled by. And the men and women on those trucks waved back, as if to say, "Hey, no problem."

This great state rolled up its sleeves, looked terrorism straight in the face, and spat in its eye. Ladies and gentlemen, I give you New York.

The crowd stood on its feet and erupted in applause. I was overcome with emotion looking out into the massive sea of people. As I stood in front of fellow Republicans, I had hoped that Democrats watching on television would also hear my appeal for unity.

I paused.

Then, I delivered words that still ring true today:

On that terrible day, a nation became a neighborhood. All Americans became New Yorkers.

And we did. America was united, undivided, and bonded together by a common dream, a common thread, and common ideals.

With so many Americans watching that evening, I also wanted to express gratitude on behalf of the entire state.

So, what I've wanted to do for a long time was to say thank you, in front of our country, and with our children watching. Thank you, America, from the very bottom of New York's heart.

I still carried the weight of lives lost, families torn apart, and the country still suffering years later. I wanted so much to reclaim the unity that had set in right after the attacks. I wanted to bring people together.

Sadly, that didn't happen. While many appreciated my words, my attempt, and my passion, Americans had already split and planted their flags. Sides had been chosen. The "you're either with us or against us" attitude continued and dominated.

While Rove's 2004 strategy worked, it came with the price of bitter division. Both Democrats and Republicans ran polarizing campaigns and left the vast middle up in the air. Bush had the chance to call for unity and win with a significant mandate. I still believe that if he had, he would have been reelected without the overwhelming negativity. Instead, he got the position for four more years, but with an enormous political divide. The campaign stoked fears, fostered anger, and built up resentment. I'm glad he won, but I wish it had been achieved in a far different manner.

In the 1930s, George Gallup started presidential approval rating polls. Shortly after 9/11, President Bush held the highest approval ratings of any modern president. He still holds the highest approval rating of any president *ever*, peaking at 90 percent. For perspective, John F. Kennedy, who was adored by the public, held 83 percent at one point. Ronald Reagan, who wiped his opponent off the map in his reelection, hit a high of only 71 percent.

Over the next few years, Bush's approval ratings slid. When he wrapped up his second term, he left with some of the lowest ratings of any modern president.

Heading into the presidential election of 2008, with a divided and angry American public, the Democratic political machine fell behind Hillary Clinton to run for its presidential nomination. But it was not her destiny. Democrats did something Democrats often do. As the political saying goes, "They don't fall in line; they fall in love." They fell hard. So did many Independents and quite a few Republicans.

Enter Barack Obama.

> We have never been just a collection of individuals or a collection of red states and blue states. We are, and always will be, the United States of America.
>
> —Barack Obama's victory speech, Chicago, 2008

I campaigned for Obama's rival, Republican nominee John McCain. But after four polarizing years, Barack Obama came in as a breath of fresh air. No one could deny his appeal. He passionately and convincingly played up themes of unity, hope, and optimism.

In terms of raw politics, his approach was brilliant. Candidate Obama's leftist ideology turned out his base, while his positive, inclusive rhetoric appealed to the broader public. Undeniably, he was the right candidate at the perfect time.

As some on the right raged with anger against President-elect Obama, I was hopeful but cautious. Many of his speeches, his words, and his themes were inspiring. I was eager to see how Obama would govern, and I thought that he could have been a transforming and uniting figure. I gave him a chance and thought Republicans should, too.

Some did. Others did not, unfortunately in sometimes vile ways. Prominent media mogul Donald Trump led "birther" attacks, questioning where Obama was born. Conspiracy theorists followed, often attacking the president with overtly racial overtones.

I wondered, *Is this the new norm?*

In the first few months of Obama's presidency, as much as I had hoped for the best, I too began to doubt him. Something that immediately rubbed me the wrong way was his trip to Cairo, Egypt, where he gave a now infamous speech apologizing for America and American interests. It was disheartening, to say the least. It was as if he had forgotten World War II, the Marshall Plan, and even that the United States had stood with Egypt during the Suez Crisis. Why did America need to apologize? Obama blamed the US for decades of foreign governments' local and regional incompetence and complicated history. It turned me off.

His leadership on policy at home became polarizing, divisive, even punitive.

My high hopes for President Obama were dashed. Obama is a man who knows the academic and the leftist political worlds really well, but not the worlds of average Americans.

Legislatively, Obama rammed through a bogus "stimulus" program, which ended up failing. Then, against more than half of Americans' wishes, came the controversial Obamacare. Never before had a policy creating such a massive entitlement been passed by only one party. Of course, this was coupled with lies about Americans being able to keep their doctors and health insurance policies. His agenda was not about advancing confidence, unity, or trust; it was about advancing government control over health care.

> **We have to pass the bill so that you can find out what is in it.**
> —Nancy Pelosi at the 2010 Legislative Conference for National
> Association of Counties, March 9, 2010

Well, that's a heck of a way to pass a law affecting nearly every single American and radically changing the health-care industry *forever*. Obamacare, technically called the Patient Protection and Affordable Care Act, was ramrodded through Congress.

This major piece of legislation was one of the first prominent examples of President Obama's breaking a big promise—a commitment to transparency. Just as the Obama administration eventually earned a reputation for hiding and disguising its foreign policy, such as drone strikes and clandestine operations around the world, Obamacare was passed with backroom deals to protect vulnerable Democrats. The senators of Nebraska and Louisiana were offered special breaks on Medicaid expansion and extra federal funds. These shady deals earned nicknames like "the Cornhusker Kickback" and "the New Louisiana Purchase." Those politicians knew that their constituents, like the majority of Americans, either didn't want government intervention in health care or simply wanted Congress to slow down, be more transparent, and debate this massive piece of legislation.

As for the president, I wanted to see more of the Obama who often indicated he was ready and willing to work with Republicans. That didn't happen, though. I was disappointed. But my feelings paled in comparison to those of millions of other Americans.

Obamacare, stimulus spending, and even a rant by CNBC reporter Rick Santelli—who asked, "How many of you people want to pay for your neighbor's mortgage?"—inspired the so-called Tea Party movement.

In 2010, I felt a political energy in America like never before as I was campaigning across the country for House and Senate candidates during President Obama's first midterm election. It was powerful. People were angry with lifelong Washington Republicans, all of the congressional Democrats, and President Obama.

The press and Democrats called it a fake movement—Astroturf not grassroots. How wrong they were. I created an organization to campaign against Democrats in the House who had voted for Obamacare. It was our sole issue. We were active in forty-four House districts. In every one, all forty-four of the Democratic incumbents lost. The anger of Middle America toward Obamacare was real. That anger changed the direction of the country radically.

The House flipped Republican, and eventually, so did the Senate. Governorships in blue states turned red. And Republicans had the greatest number of state legislators *ever*.

Quite a few newly elected senators and representatives at the state and federal levels had no political experience at all. This also signified the kind of radical change people were demanding. In 2010, the typical dynamic of the incumbent's having huge advantages over any challengers was flipped. Now, incumbency was a liability. If you were in office, you were part of the problem. Lack of political experience became an asset. Many of these new members of Congress spouted fiery rhetoric. It's fair to say that these political neophytes laid the foundation for a certain prominent businessman with no political experience to get elected to the White House years later.

Washington politics were heated throughout Obama's tenure. That's understandable. It always is, especially when Congress has opposing parties or a slim majority.

When Republicans took over the House in 2010, with the fury and fire of the Tea Party behind them, they put a stop to most of the Obama administration's goals. For conservatives, they were the firewall against liberal policy. In the media, they were deemed "obstructionists." But the word "obstructionists" quickly took a back seat to another one. With the nation's first African American president in office, pundits and prominent media personalities on the left boiled down policy differences between Democrats and Republicans to one thing: racism.

Nonsense! In fact, as I reflect on the Tea Party, the thousands of grassroots organizers and voters I worked with didn't care at all about race. Many resented both political parties; they were just as mad at Republicans as at Democrats. They were focused overwhelmingly on Obamacare, debt and deficits, and making sure that the power of both the White House and Congress were kept in check; they certainly were not focused on race.

Though the Bush administration had divided the country with the Iraq War and other foreign policy, it was Obama who began to divide the country based on domestic policy and, later, race.

President Obama approached certain tragic instances during his tenure totally disregarding facts, investigations, and findings. He used some of those tragedies to drive a wedge between Americans in order to further his own political aims.

The culture wars began.

* * *

STARTING WITH AN OFF-THE-CUFF COMMENT ABOUT AN INCIDENT in Cambridge, Massachusetts, in which police officer James Crowley, who is white, arrested a black Harvard professor at his home, President Obama somehow managed to turn something that probably would not have been a big deal into a nationwide cultural battle. The Cambridge Police Department had received a 911 call about a break-in in progress. Providing no context at all about what had happened, the president of the United States of America attacked the police officer for "acting stupidly." It turned out the officer's actions were completely proper. Soon after this debacle, President Obama invited the officer and professor to the White House for what became known as the "Beer Summit," a theatrical way for Obama to acknowledge he was wrong. It was shtick, a high-profile media move that was as juvenile as Obama's actions to begin with.

* * *

NEXT, LET ME ASK YOU THIS: *WHAT HAPPENED IN FERGUSON?*

You likely know the city. You may not know what state it's in. But you probably know that some terrible racially charged incident happened there. You are certain a white cop unjustly murdered an unarmed young black man.

Why do you think that? Because that's what we were told by the media and, indirectly, by the president and his attorney general.

Eighteen-year-old Michael Brown, an African American, was in fact shot and killed by a white officer in Ferguson, Missouri, on August 9, 2014. Upon his death, the president put out a statement that focused entirely on Brown, not the investigation or law enforcement officer.

He wrote, "The death of Michael Brown is heartbreaking, and Michelle and I send our deepest condolences to his family and his community at this very difficult time."

The president added, "I know the events of the past few days have prompted strong passions, but as details unfold, I urge everyone in Ferguson, Missouri, and across the country to remember this young man through reflection and understanding."

The comforting words are understandable and warranted. However, there were no words for the officer or police department.

The president dispatched Attorney General Eric Holder to Ferguson. The AG put out a press release saying that he had spoken to Brown's family "not just as Attorney General, but as a father with a teenage son myself." He added, "They, like so many in Ferguson, want answers." He too made it personal and about Brown.

A few days later, President Obama sent three White House officials to Brown's funeral. Yet he gave no encouragement (symbolic or otherwise) to support local law enforcement, which, by the way, was dealing with riots at the time. News of this terrible shooting spread, but not the facts. The story became a nationwide symbol of racial injustice and police brutality.

From all this, you'd have to assume Michael Brown was an innocent victim and the white cop guilty of a criminal act. The media certainly did.

The phrase, "Hands up, don't shoot," was adopted at protests against law enforcement around the country. The slogan came from the statement of an "eyewitness" who said Brown had raised his hands in the air. The phrase became a hot commodity, slapped on T-shirts and on goods sold online, and chanted at protests.

While reporting the story, one night the entire CNN news desk raised their arms in a "hands up" pose, signifying, "Hands up, don't shoot." They solidified the false narrative that a violent racial injustice had taken place. They pushed the sentiment that police officers in America were trigger-happy racists.

The great divide got bigger, this time on America's racial fault line, based on a narrative that wasn't true.

Obama then sent in another team—top investigators from his own Justice Department. They would scrutinize the shooting and the department's investigation. Their findings? They determined that Brown had assaulted the officer. Brown had just committed theft, and the officer was responding to a police radio call. There was no evidence to suggest that the officer's use of force had been "unreasonable"—both local investigators and Obama's own came to the exact same conclusion. They determined that Brown had been a violent aggressor. He had reached into the car and fought with the officer over control of his gun. The officer shot him in self-defense. The eyewitnesses who made the "hands up, don't shoot" comment had lied—contradicted by numerous other eyewitnesses.

This was barely reported. Some in the public and the media wanted to believe the story that a racist white cop had shot and killed an innocent young African American. They wanted to believe it, and so did Obama's Justice Department.

* * *

DURING OBAMA'S TWO TERMS, AS VIOLENCE AGAINST POLICE OFFI-cers escalated and some on the lunatic leftist fringe were calling for the assassination of cops, the president never attended a funeral of a police officer who had died in the line of duty. There was one exception: he did attend a memorial for five Dallas police officers who had been shot in the line of duty in July 2016 by a man who claimed he wanted to kill white cops. At that memorial, *the one for five officers who had been assassinated in cold blood*, Obama lectured on "racial discrimination" and "slavery." It was neither the time nor the place for it.

In our great country, founded on the ideals of freedom and individual rights, one terrible injustice was allowed to fester from the very beginning: slavery. Two hundred thirty-some years later its evil legacy lingers in the form of discrimination and a lasting racial divide.

Barack Obama, elected as our first African American president with broad support across the racial and political spectrum, could have been an historic voice to help close that divide. He had multiple opportunities to help heal and end divisions. He had the unique capability to bring us together and to put a nail in the coffin of racial division. He didn't.

I fully understand Obama's desire, indeed his need, to speak for the black community in our country. He should have felt a legitimate obligation to stand up for mistreated African Americans, to speak out and not remain silent. There are undoubtedly too many legitimate incidents of racial discrimination against African Americans every day in our country, and too often, examples of African Americans being subjected to a different standard of justice.

The president's most important obligation was to know the facts before choosing sides and to make sure that when his administration waded into something as sensitive as race, it would get it right. On Ferguson, the administration got it wrong. President Obama and his attorney general ran with and enhanced a narrative that turned out not to be true. He deliberately chose to polarize. This was a tremendous disappointment to me. Obama could have been a transformational, unifying figure. Instead, he used his position in a way that dramatically deepened the divide among the American people.

The media continued to further the Michael Brown narrative. They did this while a city only a few hours north of Ferguson was steeped in violence.

Year after year, the media focuses on racial issues affecting a few, yet ignores the thousands of young African Americans shot and killed year after year in the city of Chicago.

> **The killing season has begun, and is destined to run its course.**
> —"Another Summer Killing Season in Chicago," *Chicago Tribune* editorial board, May 30, 2018

Chicago, a big city with Midwestern charm, friendly people, and a stunningly beautiful skyline, is one of the country's most violent cities.

In 2016 alone, the city recorded 3,550 shooting incidents, 4,331 shooting victims, and 762 murders. Chicago had more murders that year than New York City and Los Angeles combined. This is unconscionable.

The city that was once Obama's hometown became a bloodbath *during his presidency*. It set records for murders, and overwhelmingly, this was black-on-black violence. Do you think that *maybe* Obama could have taken a moment to reflect on, condemn, or question the violence in the city he had lived in and represented in his state's legislature? No. It didn't fit the narrative.

There are some inconsistencies in the Democratic Party and the media that I will never understand. While President Obama was engaged in culture wars with the tacit support of his attorney general, Eric Holder, the reality—*the cold, hard, sad reality*—was that thousands of young African American men were being slaughtered. For the life of me, I cannot comprehend how the deaths of these young men are ignored not only by the Democratic Party when talking about violence but also by the media itself. The deafening silence is atrocious.

CHAPTER 7

CUNNING, AMBITIOUS, AND UNPRINCIPLED MEN WILL BE ENABLED TO SUBVERT THE POWER OF THE PEOPLE

WHILE WE HAVEN'T EVEN GOTTEN TO PRESIDENT DONALD TRUMP yet, let's recap where we're at right now. After 9/11, the great divide began when President Bush, misled by Cheney and Rumsfeld, sent us into Iraq under false pretenses. Bush and his opponent then compounded the growing divide by running a polarizing reelection campaign focused on mobilizing the base instead of appealing to unity.

If you're a Republican reading this now you might say, "I know Pataki, and he is a RINO—a Republican in Name Only. He's certainly no conservative!"

But if you're a Democrat, you're equally as frustrated with my assessment that our great divide got even wider when President Obama rammed through Obamacare, lied to the American people, and attacked the very concerned citizens who made up the Tea Party of 2010. He then cracked open the racial divide by pushing Ferguson's false narrative.

Calling out both sides is exactly my point. To get beyond our country's divisions, we have to be honest and willing to criticize those on "our side" to find a common understanding of what is true. There were no WMDs in Iraq; millions of people lost their health insurance plan under Obamacare. Both sides are hypocritical, sometimes right and other times wrong. To move forward, beyond our divisions, we must communicate with one another and, most important, listen. We have to find common ground. Logic, dialogue, and respect are all critical if we are to again become a nation of people working together toward a better tomorrow.

We have a crisis of leadership in this country. It's illustrated daily, from the Senate and House leadership in Washington to state and local elected officials. Many of the younger politicians in our country don't know what it means to lead, because they've grown up watching adults act like petulant children. The style of "leadership" they see, learn, and emulate is finger pointing and name calling.

Leaders define a path and then build consensus. There's no consensus building today; all you see are people screaming at one another trying to bury the other side. Leaders inspire others to come with them. There's no inspiration today; there is intentional division. The divide-and-conquer mentality permeates new pieces of legislation and even minor amendments. Politicians now merely fight fights to win or lose. The politics and power come first; principles and the people follow.

Earlier I wrote, "In times of war, policy differences become treason." These days, the automatic presumption of criminality or vile purpose permeates every decision, every spat, and every news cycle. It's as if any and every decision made by elected officials, from city council members to the president, is meant to spite, attack, and destroy the other side. The media thrives on this, tossing fuel on the fire.

Simultaneously, the media has become much more tribal and partisan than ever before and, in the process, more untrustworthy than ever. We drown ourselves in echo chambers of talking points on the left and right. On the right, you read your Breitbart and watch Fox News. On the left, HuffPost, MSNBC and, depending on the day, sometimes CNN are your go-to places. And the ratings clearly reflect this. During the Bush era, MSNBC came into its own with the maniacal, insane rants of Keith Olbermann. Fast-forward to the Obama years, when an entire prime-time lineup of talking heads on Fox became household names.

Members of Congress once held hands singing "God Bless America" after the attacks of 9/11. Now many of us can't have civil conversations with our family members, not even during the holidays. Left- and right-leaning news organizations put out articles every year around November and December along the lines of "How to Deal with Your Crazy Conservative Grandfather at Thanksgiving," or "Ways to Shut Down your Liberal Hippie Uncle on Christmas." (Side note: Maybe, *just maybe*, it isn't the grandpa or uncle but the people those stories are directed at who are the idiots.)

The news cycle instigates and fosters a climate of hate and anger that doesn't last for the day or even the hour. It lasts in characters, by the tweet.

Take any hot topic dominating the news cycle and you'll find people picking sides before all the facts are even out. Somehow the most mundane topics become *us versus them*, Republicans versus Democrats, liberals versus conservatives. People are forced to choose sides, sometimes over the dumbest nonissues.

Worse, now even if some kid gets fame with a funny Snapchat or Instagram post, or a singer has a hit song, immediately people want to know: "Where do you stand politically? Who are you, and what's your history?"

Up until 2018, Taylor Swift caught flak from the left for not making any political statements or condemning President Trump. Yes, we are talking about the enormously talented pop star Taylor Swift, sometimes known as T-Swizzle among legions of fans known as Swifties. Again, to be abundantly clear, people gave her crap for *not* talking about politics. Sure enough, she caved.

Swift, who was born and raised in Pennsylvania, endorsed the Democratic nominee for US Senate running in…Tennessee. I'm not sure what T-Swizzle's qualifications are to make political endorsements, but she does make great music.

My shopping buddy Bobby De Niro also got in on the action. The Manhattan-raised city boy got a little more Brooklyn, going on camera to call President Trump a "punk," a "dog," and a "pig." He wrapped up his tirade with, "I'd like to punch him in the face." Wow! He wasn't even in character!

In the meantime, musicians like Kid Rock and Bruce Springsteen (who are political opposites) have become toxic and polarizing simply because they may favor a candidate, party, or policy. Issues that would seemingly be beyond politics quickly show how blindly partisan so many of us are, quick to choose one side or the other. I try to ignore it all and just enjoy good music.

A powerful movement that should have remained above the political fray is #MeToo. The movement did more than any other to expose the disgusting circumstances women have been forced into for generations. Few movements have had the success of #MeToo, tangibly, legally, or culturally.

The movement has liberated women all over the country to stand up and expose the cultures they were working in, many run by power-hungry, sexually dominant male pigs. Powerful men were exposed as abusers and sexual assaulters. High-profile firings of news anchors, media moguls, and powerful executives became commonplace for months.

Although these men are considered innocent until proven guilty in a court of law, for many, the allegations that came in were consistent and convincing enough for businesses to take action. Some of the accused readily admitted they had crossed lines; others gave convoluted answers without ever explicitly denying their behavior.

The #MeToo movement also exposed the hypocrisy of the left. Countless numbers of high-profile men who engaged in abusive behavior were the same ones who preached tired and vile talking points, claiming Republicans were anti-women. These pigs claimed they were male feminists, proud to "stand with her," meaning Hillary Clinton in her campaign for president.

Speaking of Clinton, no other high-ranking Democrat did more damage to the credibility of the #MeToo movement than she did. In October 2018, as the hype around the movement began to fade, Clinton gave an interview to CBS News reporter Tony Dokoupil. Questioning her about Bill Clinton's sexual relations with Monica Lewinsky when he was president, Dokoupil said, "There are people who look at the incidents of the '90s and they say, a president of the United States cannot have a consensual relationship with an intern. The power imbalance is too great." Hillary Clinton, a self-proclaimed champion of women's rights, cut the reporter off and finished his thought for him.

"Who was an adult. But let me ask you this: Where's the investigation of the current incumbent against whom numerous allegations have been made and which he dismisses, denies, and ridicules?"

Deflecting to Donald Trump didn't serve the former First Lady well. The American public, regardless of party affiliation, recognized her hypocrisy and pathetic attempt to steer the conversation away from the issue.

When the #MeToo movement started and credible allegations surfaced, it didn't matter what social or political position the person held—there were consequences. As there should be. The movement started with the greatest intentions, and it accomplished much, raising awareness and holding powerful men accountable. Hopefully, it will accomplish much more.

But sure enough, it took a turn into politics. The #MeToo movement became weaponized as a tool, applying to people in one tribe or the other. When Democratic National Committee Deputy Chair

Keith Ellison was accused of domestic abuse, Republicans attacked. Yet he faced no blowback from his party. At about the same time the allegations against Ellison surfaced, another high-profile fight started, with sexual assault allegations dating back to the 1980s.

Senator Sheldon Whitehouse (D-Rhode Island): "Judge, have you—I don't know if it's 'boufed' or 'boofed'—how do you pronounce that?"

Brett Kavanaugh: "That refers to flatulence. We were sixteen."
—Confirmation hearings for Supreme Court Justice Nominee Brett Kavanaugh, September 27, 2018

Before we get to the brazen political calculations and character assassination of Brett Kavanaugh, it's important to clearly illustrate how the #MeToo movement played out for the overwhelming number of men accused of assault. The men who were outed for their despicable behavior faced consequences from companies where corporate boards or bosses found the allegations credible, including being fired from their jobs. Some of the men went on to face criminal charges, giving the accused and the accusers their day in court. But when a movement morphs into a political weapon to advance an agenda, things like credibility and due process don't matter.

The Supreme Court confirmations for Brett Kavanaugh took a turn so partisan, so outrageous, and so over the top that the writer for Netflix's *House of Cards* would have had a script based on them rejected for being too ludicrous. At one point, the center of debate was a thirty-something-year-old calendar that the teenage Kavanaugh used to document his social life. His scribble, along with nicknames like "Squee" and terms like "boof," got admitted into the public proceedings for debate.

The accusation—the *decades-old* accusation from a high school party—wasn't corroborated, and the accuser's own story changed repeatedly. Her "best friend" and "eyewitness" actually denied ever being there and doubted the incident ever happened. For this, she was pressured and threatened to change her memory. Yet Democrats still went to war, accusing Kavanaugh of being a gang rapist and "evil."

This type of behavior and outlandish over-the-top political maneuvering has led only to congressional approval ratings getting even lower than in years past—falling somewhere between having hemorrhoids and having an arm amputated.

People who dare question their own side also get castigated quickly. Take, for example, lawyer Alan Dershowitz, who describes himself as a liberal who voted for Hillary Clinton. One generation may know him as part of the "dream team" of lawyers who represented O. J. Simpson in the trial for murdering his ex-wife, but for decades, Dershowitz was described by most major media outlets as an outspoken "liberal lawyer." These days, Dershowitz is either an evil political shill for Donald Trump or a good man and solid supporter of the president because he had the audacity to question the legitimacy of special counsel Robert Mueller's probe into the Trump campaign.

On the right, Bill Kristol, a conservative political analyst and founder of *The Weekly Standard*, was a Never Trumper early on. Once revered by the right, now he's considered a sellout and might as well be a *darn liberal*! Dershowitz and Kristol are as loved and hated as the New England Patriots, depending on who you ask, on which day, and in what hour.

What has breaking the ranks of their sides earned them? Dershowitz can't visit his standby vacation spot on Martha's Vineyard, a liberal bastion, without catching flak from locals. *Into exile, you leper!* Meanwhile, Kristol has cemented the fact that he'll never be allowed on Fox News again. *Have fun with Rachel, Chris, or Joe at MSNBC, buddy!*

These men strayed from the tiny little boxes their tribes had put them in: *You can't do that!* As tribe members, we expect people to fall in line, think like us, act like us, talk like us. When you have a country that aligns itself into two monolithic organizations, with no gray area, no room for movement, and no room for moderation, everyone and everything becomes "part of the problem." Soon, entire institutions crumble.

They are.

Crumbling.

Right now.

The breakdown of trust among institutions goes far beyond politics and media. Is there any American institution that is not politicized? Left versus right, us versus them, with us or against us—these are now intrinsic parts of American society. This is now our culture.

From pop culture to sports to sacred institutions, everything is now partisan or politicized to use as leverage. Formerly trusted pillars of American society simply don't exist anymore. So many of us have lost our faith in just about everything, including academia, financial institutions, the church, law enforcement, the courts, media, the House, the Senate, and the White House. The list goes on and on.

We are a divided people, and the leaders of our country—aided and abetted by a media frenzy—have created it, fostered it, and thrived on it. It's a shame. To paraphrase Hillary Clinton and George W. Bush again, everything has become *us versus them*, being with us or against us.

* * *

BY THE TIME OBAMA'S SECOND TERM ENDED, AMERICAN CULTURE felt fractured beyond repair, as divided as ever. The great hope was that he would mend race relations and bring people together, but his administration did the opposite. Racial tensions raged. And in those eight years, President Obama also managed to divide the country socioeconomically, stoking anger among different classes.

For the first time, a president demonized economic success, something Americans have always strived for. Now, success was something to resent. America—the wealthiest nation on earth, with the largest middle class in the history of civilization—quickly turned into the haves and have-nots, or worse, a country run by conspiring, evil 1 percenters. President Obama's rhetoric, saying he would "spread the wealth" or telling businesses owners, "You didn't build that," fueled anger and resentment. The years of polarization left a huge segment of society feeling left out, abandoned, and angry.

In 2008, the political pendulum swung from the solemn previous couple of years under the Republican Bush administration to the seemingly optimistic Democratic nominee Obama winning the White House and holding his party's Congress. Then, in 2010, public sentiment swung once again, putting Republicans in control of the House in huge numbers. Although this was largely ignored by the mainstream media, House Republicans attempted to compromise and negotiate with the Obama administration on all sorts of issues. None of it mattered. Whatever they did, Republicans were deemed the "party of no." The public disagreed. Soon after, the Senate went Republican.

It seemed that the country's political pendulum was swinging left and right, but it never gravitated toward the center. Wildly, violently, it jerked left to right, back and forth.

As Obama was wrapping up his second term, candidates launched their campaigns to succeed him. Some candidates, like Hillary Clinton, were lost. She had no clear message whatsoever. Bernie Sanders fought for socialism even as Venezuela, which had tried the same, descended into Dante's circles of hell. Meanwhile, some Republicans and their friends and their neighbors and their siblings and their cousins twice removed all announced their candidacy, seeking the nomination. This onslaught of candidates included former governors (myself included), sitting governors and senators, and people with no political experience at all, including

Doctor Ben Carson, former CEO Carly Fiorina, and this other guy, Donald Trump.

This election season wasn't like any of those in the recent past. It seemed as if the pendulum was swinging in the proverbial political winds with no direction at all.

It wasn't left. It wasn't right.

It was all Trump.

CHAPTER 8

BEING A POLITICIAN IS A POOR PROFESSION; BEING A PUBLIC SERVANT IS A NOBLE ONE

Shit. I know shit's bad right now, with all that starving bullshit, and the dust storms, and we are running out of french fries and burrito coverings. But I got a solution.

—President Camacho in the movie *Idiocracy*

This very expensive GLOBAL WARMING bullshit has got to stop. Our planet is freezing, record low temps, and our GW scientists are stuck in ice.

—Donald Trump on Twitter, January 1, 2014

THE PRIMARY RACE FOR THE 2016 REPUBLICAN PRESIDENTIAL NOMInation was an insane combination of a Hunter S. Thompson novel and a prequel to the movie *Idiocracy*. In that movie, the entire country regresses—socially, educationally, and politically—to the point where people can't speak in complete sentences. Every other word is an f-bomb or referencing a bowel movement, and the entire population is malnourished because food has stopped growing. The reason: totally submissive to TV and marketing, people water their crops with electrolyte- and sugar-fueled sports drinks instead of water.

In a May 2016 *Time* magazine article, the writer of *Idiocracy* told journalist Joel Stein that the movie came true, except he was off by a few hundred years. In the same interview, actor Terry Crews, who plays President Camacho, claimed Donald Trump stole his character. Reflecting on the presidential debates, he said, "These people are actually talking about each other's wives. It's not politics. It's like 'Yo mama.'" Reflecting on Donald Trump specifically, he said, "The cult of masculinity has gone amok. What he is saying is, I will beat you down and take your women."

It's true. Donald Trump may have changed campaigning forever, and not for the better. Love him or hate him, allow me to share some of my personal experiences with "The Donald" to better illustrate how he steered the country politically.

Trump was first my constituent and then my opponent when I ran for president.

* * *

AFTER WINNING MY FIRST CAMPAIGN FOR GOVERNOR, WHICH WAS a major upset, I got a call.

"Hi, George. It's Donald Trump. I'm calling to say congratulations."

"Hello," I said politely, yet I was suspicious. I knew he was calling to say more than "congratulations." My finance team had called him dozens of times that fall, looking for support. He never called back.

Donald Trump then said something that just about every candidate ever in the history of politics always hears: "George, I was there with you from the beginning. I knew you were going to win, pal!"

Right! If he could only see my head-shaking smirk through the phone, as if I were foolish enough to believe him. For weeks my campaign team had called Trump's, trying to get a donation. He never called back.

"George, did you get my check?"

"What's that, Donald? A check?" I said in a very serious tone.

"Yeah. I sent it last week. Maxed out. Did you get it?"

"Well, I wouldn't know. My finance team takes care of all of that."

Then, Donald Trump, someone who can somehow always make a weird moment weirder, said, "Well, hold on just a second."

Through the phone, I could clearly hear him rifling through papers. It was so loud, it was as if he had set the phone down directly next to the papers and started tossing the entire stack around, which, by the way, was probably what he was doing. Then he came back.

"That damn secretary. I'm gonna have to fire her!" (And this was well before he was firing people from *The Apprentice*!)

Trump tried to lamely, slowly, painfully explain. "She didn't get the check out last week. She just had it delivered this morning." (This was the day after the election, by the way!)

Shaking my head in disbelief and unable to wipe the smirk off my face, as politely as I could, I said, "Sure, Donald."

That afternoon, my campaign finance office told me they got the check for the maximum donation. It was dated the week before.

Let's be clear here. That's not "quintessential" Donald Trump; that *is* Donald Trump.

* * *

ON MAY 28, 2015, IN FRONT OF A DIVERSE CROWD OF SEVERAL hundred people, I announced in both English and Spanish, "I'm running for president." We held the launch in Exeter, New Hampshire. We picked the location because it is historically significant, tied to President Lincoln. New Hampshire is also the second state that candidates go through on the road to earning their party's nomination in the primary. Iowa is first.

From the time of my first elected position as mayor of my hometown (Peekskill, New York), I loved to serve, and I often sought higher office because I wanted to do good things for my community and our country. America had given so much to my family and so many opportunities to my children, considering running for president was a way for me to give back. While intentions are good, accomplishments are what matter, and I was proud of my record as governor of New York.

In politics, the best servants for the job understand how to lead, when to listen, when to work with others, and when to follow. It's also important to make sure confidence doesn't turn into cockiness or an overinflated ego.

Overinflated egos led to Democratic nominee Hillary Clinton's taking a presidential nomination for granted and losing in a huge way. President Donald Trump has such a massive ego that it interferes with his accomplishing even the most basic goals or, worse, causes him to disaffect his own party. Egos also often lead to ideologues. Those are the worst kind of politicians, who preach about purity and who talk down to you about what you need but can't get it done. This applies to liberals who force social agendas or socialist economic policies down your throat with the heavy hand of the government and to politicians on the right who tell you everything they'll get done while saying no to everything. Ideologues talk the talk but never walk the walk.

Having led one of the most diverse states in the nation economically and culturally, I was confident I could take my skill set to Washington and accomplish great things for the country. My record would speak for itself.

When I was first elected as governor, I took a nearly insolvent state from the brink of bankruptcy to having a steady economy and then eventually to having a booming economy. I did so with fiscally conservative principles, namely tax cuts—more cuts than any of my predecessors, in fact. During my time in office, I enacted over $147 billion worth of cuts, more than all of the other forty-nine states combined, yet I left the state with billions in surplus and almost seven hundred thousand new private sector jobs. Under my tenure, Standard & Poor's boosted the state's credit rating three times, including after the economic collapse post-9/11. This was a very real reflection of the great work we were doing in Albany.

I also understood the consequences of health care in our state—or, better said, the lack of health care. While I know that Obamacare was and is a disaster, government can and should play a role in ensuring that its citizens have adequate access to health care. But there's a big difference in what I believe compared to what liberals believe. I believe in as much local control as possible, as well as private sector involvement and competition. Why would anyone want to hand off something as intimate as a relationship with a doctor to politicians in Washington?

What I did was focus on expanding care to the poorest. Over the years, I enacted laws ensuring coverage to low-income adults who could not get health insurance through an employer. We also identified gaps in Medicaid. Many New Yorkers didn't qualify for the federal insurance but had enormous trouble affording the rising costs of private insurance. We made sure they had the opportunity to be covered as well. To me, this type of leadership and policy was as conservative as it was compassionate.

A serious presidential candidate should be able to show three things: a track record proving they can lead, a vision of where they want the country to go, and the ability to win the election. Having transformed New York and won by the two largest landslides for a Republican ever in the state, I knew I had these qualities. I knew my record could contend with that of any of the candidates running for president. Sure, some of the candidates were great people, but a few had only short careers as junior senators in Washington, with a track record of doing nothing except saying no. It's not exactly hard to say no when you're a Republican refusing to go along with President Obama's agenda. That's not experience at all. Heck, although some of those young senators voted and presented themselves as ideological leaders in Washington, they barely qualified as ideologues. In their short careers, they never even had the opportunity to show what they stood for—only what they stood against. Other candidates had no experience in politics at all.

On the campaign trail, I was confident that my successful conservative record would hold sway in the eyes of both the media and the American public. Not only did I have the accomplishments, but I also had been elected to position after position as an underdog and as a Republican. I finished my career as a three-term conservative Republican governor in one of the most Democrat-dominated states in the nation. I was also proud of having high approval ratings throughout my career.

When it came to leadership, I worked hard and knew how to work well with others, even if that sometimes meant flexing a political muscle here or there. In the bare-knuckle, rough-and-tumble politics of New York, I was able to oversee the crafting of fiscally conservative budgets, an improved tax code, and a return to law and order, which wasn't easy during the especially turbulent latter half of the 1990s. Our dramatically different policies turned New York from one of the most dangerous places in the nation into the safest large state in the country, the fifth safest overall in fact. This was a massive transformation.

With my résumé, conservative credentials, and length of time as governor, I thought I was well-equipped to grow strong in the Republican primary. If I worked hard enough and was fortunate enough to make it to a general election, I was ready to dominate it, especially if the Democrats' candidate was the flawed, anointed, and crowned Hillary Clinton. After all, three times I had been elected Republican governor of New York, *a state with over two million more registered Democrats than Republicans.* I thought the general election might be easier than the primary.

Oh, how right I was; it just wasn't for my candidacy!

The campaign was in full swing. I put my track record proudly on display. I felt confident out of the gate. In the first few weeks, my polling was solid. But what I would witness shortly after, during the march toward the Republican primary, was nothing short of insane, like a car wreck really. And with this car wreck, not only did you have to slow down, but you had to come to a full stop and watch intently.

During the Republican debates, there was plenty of carnage. There was more blood spilled than in a *Night of the Living Dead* movie. It was a street fight like no one could have ever imagined—not the candidates, not the media, not the American people.

Our campaign rolled through the summer. In between eating funnel cake at the Iowa State Fair and chowing down at the Barley House in New Hampshire, I had to make calls. Lots and lots of calls. I had to undertake one of the toughest, most god-awful responsibilities on the campaign trail. I had to raise money. Tons of it.

Fund-raising is the most exhausting and soul-sucking thing you do in a campaign. Without it, though, you go nowhere fast. Being a candidate for office is a lot like being a product in the private sector. You have to package, brand, market, and sell yourself. You have to pay your staff, pay for travel, and get your face and message on TV and radio and in print and digital media. You have to be everywhere, as much as possible, at all times, including when you're not there. You spend hours and hours on the phone asking for money; this is often referred to as "dialing for dollars."

My fund-raising calls had some success, enough to build a team and start the fight, but too often they ended with the same frustrating response. Men and women I had known for decades, who had supported me through multiple races in New York, all had the same answers when I asked for their support: "I'm sorry, I gave to Jeb," or "I loved his father," or "His brother helped me." I would hear these lines over and over. Though I had loyal donors, many of them had generational ties to the Bush family.

It was at this point in the campaign that I began to realize a perfect storm was brewing. It was a storm with strong winds, setting in motion the rise of Donald Trump.

With the race for the Republican nomination being so crowded, everyone was scrambling for media exposure but not getting much.

Most of it was divided among the many candidates, with the rest of it dominated by Trump. Many of us were frantically searching for campaign contributions but getting only crumbs, not even a slice of the pie. Some of us who had the same position of governor were dividing up the same type of donor and voter base. That included Bobby Jindal, Jeb Bush, Chris Christie, John Kasich, and myself. As for the senators, including Rick Santorum, Rand Paul, Marco Rubio, and Ted Cruz, they too were taking away from one another's donor and voting bases. Even subsets of people were taking away from each another in bizarre ways. Carly Fiorina and Ben Carson were at odds, sharing a few of the same types of voters who desperately craved an "outsider."

Then the race got stranger. Bush, who raised more than one hundred million dollars, wasn't doing well in the polls. You'd think he would spend money on himself, boosting his brand and getting out his message. Nope. Instead, he spent millions attacking Marco Rubio, *who was also doing terrible in the polls.* Bush feared Rubio might steal his "momentum" or peel off "his" Florida voters. But Bush had no momentum...or Florida voters.

Adding to the madness, there was also brand confusion. Rubio was also dealing with Cruz. As young Cuban Americans with family success stories, they were so close in policy and brand, I thought they might try to off each other in a dark hallway at the next debate. Meanwhile, Christie hit Rubio. Cruz hit Bush. The crowds went after the moderators. It was crazy. Then the debates became like a bloody WWE cage match!

Everyone was hitting everyone, except one person—Donald Trump. No one dared lay a hand on him. Except me.

Why, though? *Why wouldn't anyone go after the man who consistently polled the highest among the candidates?*

One reason is, they were scared. Fellow candidates watched the wide-eyed, fascinated, drooling, nonstop coverage by the media. The more fuel Trump flung on the raging fire of the primary, the more the media filmed the pyromaniac. The more insane his statements became, the more the media put a microphone in his face. The more nicknames he came up with for opponents, the more the media repeated them. Candidates knew if they took him on, he would destroy them with a fury they had never felt before in even their most brutal races.

Donald Trump soon became like Joe Pesci's character Nicky in the movie *Casino*. In the film, Robert De Niro plays Sam Rothstein. Speaking about his partner in crime in the movie, Rothstein says, "You beat Nicky with fists, he comes back with a bat. You beat him with a knife, he comes back with a gun. And you beat him with a gun, you better kill him, because he'll keep comin' back and back until one of you is dead." The candidates knew the same thing about Trump, and they lived in fear of him.

There was another—now shocking—reason no one would attack candidate Trump. Everyone, *and I mean everyone*, was absolutely, thoroughly convinced he would eventually drop out of the race. No one would attack him or question him because they were certain he would dip in the polls and quit at some point. And whenever he did drop out, they would beg like puppies for his endorsement.

Never happened.

The winds of the perfect storm continued to whip up something fierce as the debates got underway. A hurricane was on the horizon.

* * *

WHEN IT WAS TIME TO GO TOE-TO-TOE WITH THE OTHER CANDI-dates in the debates, I was ready. I was prepped. I was excited. Then quite a few of us had our bubbles burst. The cable networks announced perhaps the most ridiculous rule in modern history for the presidential debates. They would divide up the candidates based on quick initial polling, placing some candidates in a first tier for a prime-time debate and others in a second tier for an earlier debate. The decision had nothing to do with track records, experience, or history. It was based entirely on name identification, which determined standing in the polls at that time.

Let me make the consequences of this as clear as possible. What this rule meant was that someone like Donald Trump—with no experience in government or politics whatsoever but with a hit TV show and his name stuck on tall buildings, crappy steaks, awful vodka, and even a cologne described by Estée Lauder as a "fragrance experience" for thirteen bucks that emanated "notes of mint, citrus, basil, cucumber, green notes, wood, and vetiver"—would easily have access to the prime-time debates.

With this logic of using name ID to place first- and second-tier candidates, surely Kim Kardashian would have been placed on the main stage. How about Kid Rock, Kanye West, Howard Stern, or the Rock? No way those guys would run, though, right? If they did, they'd be on the main stage.

The news got worse. The next thing I knew, I got relegated to the second tier of the debates, which would be aired on TV but before the main debate. In no time at all, the second-tier debate was labeled "the kiddie table."

Picture it. It's Thanksgiving. The adults point me in the direction of the table that hovers all of one foot off the ground. It has tiny pink and blue toy stools surrounding it. I demand to know, "How do you expect me to sit here? I'm six-foot-five and 225 pounds!" Still, I sit down and have awkward silences with distant cousins Rick Santorum and Carly Fiorina. I don't pout like a kid, but there is a reason to be frustrated.

I was a Republican governor who had won over a massively Democratic state for three terms and had a strong résumé backing up my work. I had overseen and helped lead a state that had an economic output the size of the entire country of Canada. And when I was in the position of governor, I didn't bail out like Mitt Romney after a few failed years. Nor did I get elected with an inherited last name, like Bush. Hell, I didn't even have my name on steaks or cologne that had notes of vetiver! And for God's sake, can anyone please tell me, *what the hell is vetiver*? I don't know. What I do know is that I had a tangible record of success and thought it should have counted.

In the debates, I made an immediate, fatal mistake: I followed the rules. I should have known better, but it's how I was raised. Evading, ignoring, and breaking the rules would have served me much better.

South Carolina Senator Lindsey Graham is a great example of someone I should have followed. When he got a question, it went something like this:

"Senator, what's your position on more taxes on the wealthy?"

"Iraq."

"*What?*"

"Yes, I've been to Iraq ninety-four times."

In seconds, the man would somehow shift the conversation into how many times he'd been to Iraq. It was ridiculous. When he was off the debate stage and answering questions from the public, the man was a robot. Maybe better said, he was like some Hollywood character actor who insists that everyone call him by his character's name even when they're not shooting the movie. He'd play the part whether or not the camera was rolling.

"Senator Graham, how's the weather?"

"In Iraq right now, it's dry, hot, and sunny. I've been there 1,345 times this year. We need to take the War on Terror abroad."

"Lindsey, it was so nice to see you reach across the aisle on that last piece of legislation. How else can we work together?"

"I'll reach across to Iraq and tear the caliphate up by the roots."

I was specifically conscious of not talking about the September 11 attacks over and over. I didn't want to be the guy who made 9/11 a subject, verb, and object. While 9/11 undoubtedly is part of what shaped me and is a massive part of my history, it would have felt disrespectful to do that.

Needless to say, it was a tough situation. Relegated to the kiddie table, I knew it was over. I'd go through the motions in the first debates, but with no media and fewer dollars from donors, I sat back like everyone else and watched the media scream about Trump all day and night.

I don't know what the solutions should have been. I understand you can't have more than a dozen people—some with egos and mouths bigger than others—sharing a stage and talking over one another. But at minimum, they could have put some of us on the main stage for at least a debate or two for some exposure to the public. It was an unfair setup, but I don't think anything would have made a difference.

Soon the storm of divided votes, donors, and name ID whipped up to become a hurricane, wrecking everything in its path. Its name was Hurricane Trump.

> **Real tough, real tough.... I'm at forty-two, you're at three!**
> —Donald Trump laying into Jeb Bush about his low polling in the final Republican primary presidential debate of 2015, Las Vegas, Nevada

While Rubio, Cruz, and Paul debated things like debt and deficits, government surveillance and due process, Trump was lighting up audiences with raw, unadulterated—dare I say?—truth. At one point, Trump flat out said he donated money to politicians to get favors. He said he donated to Republicans, and had no qualms boldly stating he also gave to Democrats.

"I will tell you that our system is broken. I gave to many people. Before this, before two months ago, I was a businessman. I give to everybody. When they call, I give. And do you know what? When I need something from them two years later, three years later, I call them. They are there for me. And that's a broken system."

Wow!

Think about that for a second. Someone running to secure the nomination of the Republican Party openly stated that he donated money to Democrats.

In that moment, Trump did what only the best candidates and debaters do—he took his weakness and made it his strength. Trump flaunted the fact that he donated to prominent Democrats—*including the Clintons!*—and then flipped it to state something that appealed to so many Americans: *This is what's wrong with Washington! Rich people give money to get favors!*

As Bush and Kasich proudly talked about their gubernatorial records, Trump talked about his success as a businessman, employing thousands of people and building a net worth of billions. Maybe "talked" is the wrong word. He bragged. He ranted. He went off on tangents that sometimes made no sense. The crowds ate it up.

Donald Trump understands something that most Republicans do not: *it's not what you say; it's how they feel.*

Trump understands the power of emotion. Conservatives, with a political philosophy based on facts, figures, and statistics, often don't understand that, or they have a hard time expressing it in a way that touches people's hearts.

Emotion drives adoration, poll numbers, and votes. Numbers, statistics, and résumés do not.

With his star appeal, his cult-like following, and his emotional drive, do you know who Donald Trump became? *A Republican type of Obama.*

Sounds crazy, right? Stay with me here.

For years, conservatives desperately searched to find their "Republican Obama," a counterweight to the powerful and well-liked liberal. Longtime political consultants—in all of their wisdom—pointed to Marco Rubio, the junior senator from Florida with a powerful backstory as a son of Cuban immigrants and a heck of a speaker. Rubio, too, could light up a room, but in a different way. Others thought it was Rand Paul, the libertarian firebrand who appealed to Democrats and young people throughout the country...allegedly.

Speakers who know how to captivate people understand that basically two emotions compel and capture people: love and hate. Obama was quintessential love, hope, and optimism. He had people lining up by the thousands to see him speak. Musicians were writing hits about him. Schools were devoting classroom songs to him. He was an icon, a beloved figure. He even won a Nobel Peace Prize just before sending drones and the military into parts of the Middle East and Africa, a result of one of the most aggressive foreign policies in years, to assassinate, capture, kill, and maim. He was "historical" before he had a history.

Then along came Donald Trump.

Not one Republican was able to captivate the people like him. Going back to the emotional play of love and hate, I'm not saying Trump is full of hate, but he had the opposite emotional effect of Obama's. He put fear into the electorate. He played on anger and resentment. Some of it was just. It was fitting, appropriate, and right.

Just as Obama was able to captivate with the feel-good language of optimism, most especially in that angry, post-Bush time frame, Trump laid out the genuine fears that many Americans struggle with every day. Undoubtedly, Trump often used horrible and pro-vocative language in describing situations and people. Some of it had disgusting racial overtones. But Trump also thoroughly under-stood people's anger, resentment, and genuine concerns about wage stagnation, jobs being decimated, the economic effects of illegal immigration, and a dysfunctional Washington.

Trump saw how much the American public despised poli-ticians, and as an outsider, he seized on it. He insulted. He gave nicknames. He bragged. He discarded every norm that political candidates follow. And the crowds loved it.

When he hit the campaign trail, he did so in a way he had done during all of his life as a businessman. He made everything "yuuuge," including his over-the-top rhetoric, his choices of words, even his hand gestures. He went big, and the crowds followed. Throngs of angry Republicans, interested Independents, and disaffected Dem-ocrats went to see Trump. Soon, they fell in love with him.

Like Obama, Trump attracted tens of thousands of people to his rallies. Fans lined up at seven in the morning for his events at seven in the evening. He commanded audiences and airtime. Donald Trump became, and still is, a Republican version of Obama.

Of course, across the spectrum you'll get all sorts of other descriptions for Trump, too. Depending on whom you ask, he's the second coming of Jesus. He's the grand wizard of the KKK. He's the best president ever, better than the high priest of conservatism, Ronald Reagan. He's Hitler reincarnated.

The truth is, he is Donald Trump—the same man I've known for decades, personally and through the lens of national and New York City media.

For years, Republicans had been searching for their star. They, at least the ones outside of the Washington Beltway and the bubble of New York City, found him. While Trump's rhetoric turned off the donor elites, it ignited the latent anger that seethed across America's heartland. Trump didn't only shake up norms; he destroyed them. At absolutely no point in the debates did he ever let up. He didn't pump the brakes for a second. Soon came the nicknames.

"Little Marco." *Ouch.* "Lyin' Ted Cruz." *Wow!* "Low-Energy Jeb." *Oh, that hurts!*

Donald Trump is someone who knows, understands, lives, and breathes marketing and branding. I have no doubt that Trump understood those two components specifically—branding and marketing—better than any candidate in the history of presidential politics. He *branded* his opponents with a hot iron of nicknames that scarred them for life, and he marketed those brands, as well as his own, at every debate. He even held press conferences to unveil and showcase new names he had come up with.

It was, and is, all so funny, so hilarious, and so sad.

During the debates, Trump repeatedly made a particular point, once again highlighting and illustrating the truth whether or not he wanted to flaunt it or the public wanted to buy it. In the last debate of 2015, Trump accused CNN of baiting his opponents: "It's very sad that CNN leads Jeb Bush, Governor Bush, down a road by starting out virtually all of the questions with 'Donald Trump.'"

He was right. He said that centering the entire debate around "Trump this, Trump that" was unprofessional. Of course, the laughable aspect is that Trump reveled in the attention.

> catch-22 (noun)—a dilemma or difficult circumstance from which there is no escape because of mutually conflicting or dependent conditions.
>
> —*Oxford English Dictionary*

Donald Trump inspires, excites, and motivates Republicans. Even more so, he motivates Democrats. We saw it in the 2018 midterms, and we may see it again in 2020.

He's a giant catch-22. If you take away Donald Trump's nicknames, bravado, and occasional lies, he doesn't get the media coverage he commanded. He doesn't win the primary. And I don't think he wins the presidency. If you take only a few of those components away, Donald Trump becomes just another boring Republican, minus experience in government. Without the over-the-top—grotesque to some, inspiring to others—personality traits, he doesn't win.

Trump saw what no other politicians did: millions of Americans, a unique voting bloc made up of Republicans, Democrats, and Independents, who wanted someone to not only shake up Washington, but to burn it down.

The past two presidential elections left many Republican voters uninspired and disappointed. Nominees like the late Senator John McCain and former Governor Mitt Romney did little to stir up or motivate large numbers of Republicans or Independents. They certainly didn't swing Democrats either.

Trump gave people something to get excited about. From his blunt positions on trade issues to the way he presented himself and spoke to crowds, Trump shook up what it meant to be a Republican while simultaneously winning over loads of Republicans and others. He shook up what it meant to be a presidential candidate and contender. He also shook up the media in a way that no one had ever seen before.

> **"A Racist, Sexist Demagogue Just Won the New Hampshire Primary: Donald Trump seriously did it."**
> —title and subtitle of an article by Ryan Grim and Igor Bobic, HuffPost, February 9, 2016

Trump refused to accept the GOP narrative that he was too inexperienced, too vulgar, and too crazy to bring together any kind of a voting bloc. After eight years of being called racist by Democrats and the media for having basic policy disagreements with President Obama, Republicans around the country were fed up with labels, too. Some Republicans who condemned his language and tone publicly, privately loved the fact that Trump was doing something few Republicans had ever attempted: hitting back.

After being called a racist on the campaign trail over and over, Trump started pointing out the hypocrisy of it all. The same people calling him a white supremacist hadn't seemed to have a problem with him a year before, when he was Donald Trump the businessman, political donor, and TV star. Hip-hop moguls, actors, and powerful prominent Democrats, like Hillary Clinton and Chuck Schumer, all loved him and took his checks. They loved his products, his hotels, and his TV shows, all until the moment he announced he was running for president as, *God forbid*, a Republican. *Gasp!*

Trump created chaos and stirred up madness. It meant clicks on websites, huge ratings on TV, and sales for declining newspapers. Trump was great for business, and the media devoted their every effort to him in unprecedented ways, giving him ink and airtime.

Earlier, I wrote that I made the mistake of following the rules in the debates. Donald Trump broke them, smashed them, and burned them to the ground, and along with them, GOP norms. Institutional Republicans reacted in horror. They were stunned.

No one knew how to respond. Anyone who tried to hit back got slapped with one of those nicknames.

For me, still at the kiddie table, I didn't even earn one. Although, after I criticized him in debates, Trump eventually lashed out at me too, saying I "couldn't be elected dogcatcher." So much for all those years of him telling the public I was one of the greatest governors New York ever had!

In the primary, Trump would go on to chew up and spit out the other candidates, with the media adoring every second of him screaming "Little Marco," "Lyin' Ted," and "Low-Energy Jeb." Hurricane Trump swept the nomination. Then he pulled off another incredible feat. He beat Hillary Clinton.

He became President Trump.

CHAPTER 9

WHATEVER YOU ARE,
BE A GOOD ONE

ONE HALF OF AMERICANS WERE SO ANGRY THAT THEY CHANNELED their resentment of Washington, DC, and political elites right through Donald Trump. In the voting bloc of Republicans, no one, not an evangelical Christian or a social conservative, seemed to care at all about morals, principles, political philosophy, or a shred of class. They wanted someone who was going to fight back.

Earlier in this book, I called out Obama on culture wars. There's no doubt Trump weirdly, awkwardly, and later definitively played into them as well. But as a Republican, he was treated radically differently by the press.

It has been obvious to me since I was a kid that if people advocate hate, regardless of the type of hate it is, you have to come down aggressively on them and marginalize them, treating them as what they are—despicable bigots or racists.

Unfortunately, many of President Trump's statements on race, immigration, and culture branded him well before he got into the White House. During his campaign, when Trump spoke out about Mexico sending "criminals" and "rapists" to the US, his racist rhetoric demonized immigrants coming in from Latin America. His horrific choice of words may not reflect the man he is inside, but it certainly became the perception.

By the time Trump became president, he was defined as a bigot. That was the narrative. And no matter what he said or did, a lot of the reporting would reflect that. Don't get me wrong: President Trump doesn't help himself when he launches into tirades, often lumping together disconnected thoughts. His ambiguous, all-over-the-place rhetoric in the wake of the white supremacist march in Charlottesville, Virginia, exemplified that.

In Charlottesville, a group of neo-Nazi, tiki-torch-wielding, khaki-pants-wearing, young white men clearly used the issue of Confederate statues as a mantle for racism to intimidate people of color. After their march, protests continued the next day and ended horrifically. A self-identified white supremacist who participated in the march rammed his car through a crowd of counter-protesters, killing a thirty-two-year-old woman.

President Trump should have immediately issued a clear rejection of the march and condemned the racists participating in them. Instead, that same day in a brief press conference, he infamously said there was "hatred, bigotry, and violence on many sides." That statement landed him in hot water with Democrats and Republicans alike, with GOP senators like Cory Gardner in Colorado and Florida's Marco Rubio taking to Twitter to slam the president. Two days later, President Trump explicitly said, "I'm not talking about the neo-Nazis and the white nationalists, because they should be condemned totally." But, once again, that statement came within an incoherent rant and amidst other comments about "very fine people on both sides."

However, President Trump, with his occasionally over-the-top and seemingly random rhetoric, sometimes gets slammed as being a racist when he's simply laying out the stark reality.

> Many Gang Members and some very bad people are mixed into the Caravan heading to our Southern Border. Please go back,

> you will not be admitted into the United States unless you go
> through the legal process.
>
> —Donald Trump on Twitter, October 29, 2018

You know, he's not wrong. For months, thousands of people from Honduras, Nicaragua, and Guatemala made their way north. Their final destination was America. The media described them as peaceful families seeking asylum, looking for safety and security away from the horrific conditions in Central America. I am certain the overwhelming majority of those migrants were good people, but I also know that Trump's statements about the caravan and criminals were true. But the left heard only racism.

Jim Acosta of CNN was a prominent voice questioning the language and semantics that President Donald Trump deployed before the 2018 midterm elections. Acosta was convinced it was racist rhetoric designed to motivate voters in the November election.

The president held a press conference shortly after the elections, as most do to either gloat or try to turn a loss into a win. Acosta began the questioning.

"As you know, Mr. President, the caravan was not an invasion. It is a group of migrants moving up from Central America towards the border with the US."

One of the very definitions of the word "invasion," by the way, is "an incursion by a large number of people or things into a place or sphere of activity."

In late November 2018, roughly five thousand migrants showed up at the US-Mexico border. Hundreds breached it, with reports of people making a run for it, dodging in and out of traffic.

The day of the press conference, Acosta finished his rant by saying, "They're hundreds of miles away. That's not an invasion."

When the caravan arrived, violence broke out. Frustrated migrants threw rocks and bottles at law enforcement on both sides of the border. Law enforcement in turn launched tear gas to break up the rowdy crowd.

MSNBC dispatched reporters to the border, doing what old-school responsible journalists do: put boots on the ground. In one hilarious example of media bias, MSNBC anchor Stephanie Ruhle, the cohost of *Velshi & Ruhle*, began tossing out loaded, politically charged questions to the reporter at the border.

Ruhle set up a premise that the caravan was made up mostly of women and children and that some of the migrants ran across the border "because they thought it was their only chance." Correspondent Gadi Schwartz shot that down quickly, saying, "From what we've seen, the majority are actually men, and some of these men have not articulated that need for asylum. Instead, they have talked about going to the United States for a better life to find work."

In March 2019 alone, more than one hundred thousand migrants arrived at the border—more than twice as many as the same month the year before. In April the record-breaking number continued, again topping one hundred thousand.

None of this vindicated Trump, though.

I'm a great believer that Latino immigration is a godsend to the United States. Having said that, when Donald Trump addressed the massive migrant caravans heading toward the United States in October 2018, he said some things that were probably true. I don't think that saying there may have been criminals and gang members within that caravan was incorrect or remotely controversial. In all likelihood, it was true; among the thousands traveling north, the odds are actually overwhelming. Yet, leftists are so blinded by their hate for Trump and yearning for open borders, they can't acknowledge that basic fact.

The president was right in saying that we cannot simply allow caravans to cross our borders. When there is an organized effort by thousands of people to simply ignore a border and cross into another country, if it is not an invasion, it is certainly a major intrusion that warrants an appropriate and significant response.

The responses of both Republicans and Democrats to the caravan are typical of the American political class today. We wait until there's a symptom and then react to it, as opposed to dealing with the actual cause of the illness. We pop an aspirin for recurring head-aches. We take Tums because we can't be bothered by acid reflux. We never treat the underlying cause, whether it's dealing with countries in Central America that are in shambles or fixing our own country's legal immigration system.

For President Trump, the caravan clearly showed the need for his wall. He saw illegal immigrants, criminals, and cartel members. Dem-ocrats saw only families and hardworking individuals who wanted to make a better life for themselves. The fact is, there are both among those seeking to cross our borders—families with the best intentions and criminals. Denying the problem serves no one's interest. Our immigration laws incentivize hundreds of thousands of people to storm our borders every month. Some have legitimate reasons, claim-ing asylum; others just want to get into our country. Sure, many want to work and make a better life for themselves, but undoubtedly, there are some who want to take advantage of the system.

Donald Trump, like so many Republican presidents and candi-dates before him, will be deemed a racist no matter what he does. Of course his rhetoric is over the top! But one of the things I always reject is making a blanket assumption that someone harbors anger or resentment against another person based on gender, religion, or race just because that person has a different viewpoint on issues. And when Democrats call Republicans bigots for wanting to secure the US-Mexico border or racist for passing a tax cut, they only lessen the importance of such charges when they are justified.

When it comes to elected leaders, we should judge them by their actions. This sentiment comes from my time as governor. Whether I pushed for legislation on the environment or on criminal justice, pundits and the media would question my actions not on the merits of the policy but on what they deemed was my underlying political motive. When I fought for cutting-edge environmental policies as governor, they assessed that it wasn't because I cared deeply about the environment but because I was trying to suck up to Democrats. The next day, another position was deemed far right and that I had taken it because I was trying to solidify my base. While I did feel strongly about certain issues that may have been perceived as being left or right, the specific policy didn't matter. Jaded cynics in the media would simply shoot it down as a politically calculated move.

I am highly reluctant to think that I can understand the inner workings of a politician's mind other than my own. But if President Trump toned down the rhetoric, he might find he'd be taken more seriously in areas of policy.

Charlottesville and Trump's language are stains on his presidency. In fact, Charlottesville and Trump's divisive, partisan, and often unnecessarily provocative rhetoric have widened our country's great divide even more. The right turns a blind eye to some of his most outrageous statements, and the left, meanwhile, has gotten so worked up by every statement, every facial gesture, and every Trump tweet that their frenzies have earned a nickname: Trump Derangement Syndrome, or TDS. TDS has even found its way into Wikipedia, defined as a "derogatory term for criticism or negative reactions to United States President Donald Trump that are irrational and have little regard towards Trump's actual positions or actions taken."

What some on the left still don't understand is that Donald Trump has tapped into a cross section of the American public like few presidents before him have.

Donald Trump ran for and won the Republican nomination and the presidency because he called out three issues and sold them in over-the-top ways. The three issues struck a chord with middle America in particular.

One, illegal immigration: "I'm going to build a wall, and Mexico will pay for it."

Two, Washington corruption: "I'm going to drain the swamp."

And three, China: "I beat the people from China. I win against China. You can win against China."

Americans are for legal immigration and are against illegal immigration. The majority of Americans do not want open borders. Trump recognized this and capitalized on it, sometimes using provocative, ridiculous rhetoric. He convinced the public that only he could stop illegal immigration and close the porous border.

As for Washington, the businessman and TV star saw the bipartisan anger directed at DC politicians. "Drain the swamp" was a way of saying, "All of these politicians are crooks. The place isn't just transactional. It is corrupt." Again, he convinced the public only he could clean it up.

Finally, no one in either party had any idea that taking on China would resonate with voters at all. It did, in a big way.

For decades, American factories had been closing and businesses had been moving thousands of good jobs to Mexico and overwhelmingly to China. Low tariffs and free-market economic orthodoxy were supposed to lead to greater prosperity. Free trade was supposed to lift us all up. Sure, maybe corporate accounting ledgers saw greater income and profits, but the unemployed factory worker in Pennsylvania or Ohio didn't. Companies' profits soared, but America's once great manufacturing powerhouse came crashing down around us. The way Trump sees it, free trade might mean you pay a dollar less for a pair of jeans at Target or fifty cents less for a hammer at Walmart, but it also means hundreds of thousands of blue-collar Americans will lose their jobs. Social and economic decay followed free trade.

Trump nailed this politically, and his bold, brash, fighting style fit the mood of those forgotten middle Americans. He was the only one who broke with Republicans on free trade orthodoxy and said it's more important to have factories in the Midwest than to save a few bucks on a product made in China. Again, he sold his message: only he could stop China from stealing our jobs.

Today, we have the lowest unemployment rate in fifty years, the lowest African American unemployment rate in recorded history, and a booming stock market. Between the tax cuts and deregulation, Trump is showing that conservative economic policy allows the private sector to do what it does best, which is grow the economy and improve people's lives.

Unfortunately, while the Trump economy is booming, so much of his success is getting lost in the incessant noise.

* * *

THE "CHAOS PRESIDENT," AS TRUMP HAS BEEN DUBBED, HAS SHOWN us that conservative economic policies can work. "What?" you may be asking incredulously. I get it. Who even knows what accomplishments Trump has had? How could we name any when we're so caught up in every tweet the guy sends as soon as he wakes up in the morning?

There's no question that Trump drives the news cycle, by the day, the hour, the minute, and by every character on Twitter. But what gets lost is that some of his conservative policy actually works. That's unfortunate.

Basic conservative policies are working: Tax cuts have had a profound effect on people's lives and the economy. Deregulation has freed up American entrepreneurship. Now, we have growth that we could have only dreamed about under a Hillary Clinton administration. And by far the largest income growth is for lower- and middle-income workers. Republican economic policies have delivered. These core economic philosophies work, just as they worked in the state of New York. Unfortunately, no one sees that they can and have, because Donald Trump overshadows absolutely everything.

Although I wasn't an enthusiastic supporter of Donald Trump's candidacy, the truth is that I want him to succeed. We had a few political battles in the presidential primary, but over the years we had an amiable relationship. In fact, he invited me to his wedding when he married his current wife, Melania.

Interestingly enough, Donald Trump's wedding reception seemed to me to be a microcosm of the environment in Washington—*entirely transactional.*

"Transactional" is a word you often hear spoken by TV political pundits or you read in the paper. Here's what it means: if you can't do something for Donald Trump, you're not really of value. You're more like nonexistent. He's a fast-paced businessman who knows exactly what he wants and how to get it done. From the beginning of his career, he has understood the power of media and the power of relationships, and he superbly works both in give-and-take ways. So, if you can do something for the Donald, you have some real value, and if you have value, you just might get wooed and invited to his wedding, reserved for his "special" and "close" friends—all 350 of them.

His "close" friends at the wedding on that special day of his third marriage included quite possibly the most random cross section of celebrities, business moguls, and powerful politicians ever assembled. It was like an *Avengers* movie with *Star Wars* characters. Not one to gawk, though, I didn't realize the amazingly diverse crowd until I took my seat in the church.

At six-foot-five, I am never the shortest guy in the room. Normally, I hover over everyone. But when I situated myself in the church pew and looked up, I couldn't see a thing. The largest human being I've ever met was smack in front of me, blocking my view. That man was Shaquille O'Neal.

Unable to see much in front of me, I looked around at the attendees. The crowd was as random as it was hilarious. Guests included Don King, the boxing promoter with his spiked hair, waving his ever-present American flag; Robert Kraft, the owner of the New England Patriots; and the rap mogul then known as Puff Daddy, soon to be P. Diddy, and after that, just Diddy. There was longtime news veteran Barbara Walters, as well as presidents of TV and cable networks, entertainment executives from New York and LA, the Clintons, and all sorts of other political players. And in this massive crowd, as I tried to get a look at Donald and Melania, all I got was a killer view of the back of Shaq's big-and-tall tailored suit.

Transactional.

While I have no doubt that many of those in attendance were true friends, undoubtedly most, like me, were there because of what they might be able to do for him in the future. Those people—from politicians to connected executives—were all currency, and Donald Trump knows exactly when and how to spend his currency and use theirs.

While I address the current president of the United States in this manner, I want to reiterate that Donald Trump is really good at what he does. He is one of the best when it comes to branding, marketing, and influencing. It's my hope that he uses those talents to lead the country in a positive direction.

As of this writing, I'm not pessimistic. I am worried. I'm concerned not for America but for its politics.

* * *

MANY OF THE POLITICIANS IN WASHINGTON ARE JUST AS TRANSACtional, and they run the gamut from the longtime party insiders to the newer, rebellious "outsiders." Many of those so-called outsiders know, understand, and play games with legislation, even when they tell you they're not in Washington "to play games."

Transactional politics aren't always bad. Sometimes they can be good when they come in the form of compromise and getting things done for the greater good. But many transactions happening in Washington and in state capitals are not for the greater good. They include transacting with lobbyists, buying and selling votes, or selling lies to the members of the public to earn their votes.

Both major parties adopt talking points based on serious issues, but often they're not serious about them at all. Sure, the parties sell them to the American public, but they're not interested in acting on them. A great example of an issue that goes in and out of fashion is our national debt. Not quite as trendy as bell-bottoms, the debt is more like cargo shorts. They're not always exactly in style, but politically, cargo shorts are like a Swiss Army knife. They can always be utilized when needed.

During the Bush presidency, when Republicans were in control of Congress, votes to raise the debt ceiling were as mundane as roll calls. Ongoing wars, an expanded Department of Education, new parts of Medicare, and all sorts of federal programs began to drive up the debt. Back then, Democrats were angry about this debt. That sounds laughable now, right?

Read this next quote. It's beautiful, politically and practically.

The fact that we are here today to debate raising America's debt limit is a sign of leadership failure. It is a sign that the U.S. government cannot pay its own bills. It is a sign that we now depend on ongoing financial assistance from foreign countries to finance our government's reckless fiscal policies. Increasing America's debt weakens us domestically and internationally. Leadership means that "the buck stops here." Instead, Washington is shifting the burden of bad choices today onto the backs of our children and grandchildren. America has a debt problem and a failure of leadership. Americans deserve better.

Well said, huh? The US senator who delivered that speech was the Tea Party-aligned fiscal hawk...um, Barack Obama. Yep. Then Senator Obama spoke out in 2006 against adding to the debt because he was super concerned about how it would affect our children and grandchildren.

Let's face it: Democrats love kids more than Republicans do!

The day Obama took office, debt went out of style as an issue for Democrats faster than faux hawks in the mid-2000s, French rolled jeans in the '80s, and bell-bottoms in the '70s. President Obama raised the national debt by almost ten trillion dollars, more than all other previous presidents combined.

For eight years, the same House Republicans who had once passed debt-ceiling votes like tossing beads at a Mardi Gras parade challenged the "fiscally irresponsible" Obama. They were furious that he was demanding more spending, so they threatened him, saying they were not going to raise the debt ceiling for his administration. They said Obama was putting that debt on the backs of our grandchildren.

Apparently, under President Obama, Republicans loved the kids more than Democrats!

Republicans used debt-ceiling votes as leverage in policy negotiations. Democrats decried them for "holding the nation hostage."

Now, with Trump in office, Republicans once again aren't batting an eye as the country's deficits hit near trillion-dollar levels.

Looks like Republicans hate kids all over again!

Both parties pick and choose what they stand for and go against depending on how it fits into their political narrative. From the divisive and irresponsible rhetoric to the cutthroat politics of Obama and Trump, and the basic dysfunction of a transactional Washington, there is a particular group that threatens our democracy, now more than ever. They're ideologues, and both parties are infected with them.

Ideologues should not be lawmakers. Period. There's a big difference between having an ideology and being an ideologue. It's important to have an ideology, and a strong one at that. But ideologues take a "burn it all down" approach that serves no one.

In Washington and on campaign trails across the country, these ideologues rail against the system, against the incumbents, and against everything else, yet they have few ideas of their own. In office they rarely, if ever, work on solutions with their fellow party members or across the aisle. Most of them vote no on *everything*. If the opposite party introduces legislation or even an idea, it's an automatic no. If party leaders introduce legislation, they tell those leaders to their face they'll think about it. Then they vote no. They reject everyone and everything. When they do, they take up the mantle of being "holier than thou," or better said, "more conservative (or liberal) than thou." In reality, they do nothing at all. They look great in fund-raising mailer photos, but they never deliver in the real world.

Ideologues don't make good leaders. They make for tolerable speakers for well-funded think tanks, getting paid to speak at Ritz-Carlton hotels and to talk to small crowds of wealthy Americans.

They reassure everyone how great America is—speaking to conservatives about no government at all or to liberals about government control of everything. On television, the more bombastic they are, the more airtime they get. On social media, the crazier their statements are, the more followers they amass. Ideologues are today's political rock stars.

Speaking of rock stars, an excellent example of media-adored ideologues today is known as "the Squad." Made up of four far-left Democratic representatives, the Squad comes branded and packaged like a hot new politically charged rock band. Alexandria Ocasio-Cortez heads up the group as lead singer. She's worshipped for her uncontrollable, over-the-top antics, and even has a nickname, AOC. On guitar, Ilhan Omar is the intense, outspoken rebel. Rashida Tlaib is the kooky bass player. Ayanna Pressley is the drummer no one knows until she speaks up, and when she does, you bet it will be provocative.

The Squad dominates TV news coverage. They grace the covers of magazines. And they are omnipresent on social media with millions of followers.

Aside from slamming Republicans as racists and Donald Trump as a white supremacist, what have they done to deserve all this attention? What bills have they passed? What realistic goals have they even proposed? Most specifically, I ask: What ideas have they advanced to improve the lives of Americans?

Today, that's not what gets media attention.

Be outrageous. Reject everything. And instead of being condemned as a fool, you will be elevated as a star.

While I'm not an ideologue, I am a conservative. What I learned in my trials and tribulations of governing is how to lead.

Leading requires more than ideological purity. It requires compromise and understanding. If you want to govern, you have to work toward solutions and solve problems with people of all political and philosophical stripes.

I know because I have.

What I learned is that being a governor or mayor is far different than being a legislator. Legislators vote—yes or no—and then move on to the next issue. In the executive branch, you have to deal with the consequences of that vote. You have to figure out how to make things work, because ultimately, as a mayor, governor, or president, you are responsible for success or failure. That's why former governors make the best presidents and so few legislators have successfully served in the White House. Legislators can be pure ideologues and avoid the consequences of their actions, vote after vote, day after day. Sure, they rally the base. Yes, they get the media excited and command TV time. But nothing happens. Only talk.

As a former Republican governor of an overwhelmingly Democratic state, I know that you accomplish goals and influence people by leading and, yes, compromising. And "compromise" is not a bad word. Meeting halfway, or better yet, getting 70 or 80 percent of what you want, if that's what it takes to move things forward, is a good thing. Being pure, but getting nothing done, is not.

Though I'm still an optimist on policy, politics, and people, I also know that we, as people, are fallible. As I harp on DC, on both the Republican and Democratic Parties, Lord knows I made plenty of mistakes in my tenure as governor. We all fail; we all get knocked down. What's important is to recognize what you've done and where you are, pick yourself up, and get back at it.

We need to do this as a country.

After the attacks of September 11, I witnessed some of the most horrific and disturbing sights that no human being should have to endure. I also witnessed the resilience and determination of some of our heroes during the absolute worst, darkest times.

* * *

"THERE...THERE ARE SOME REMAINS," YELLED A FIREMAN.

It is morning, months after 9/11. I'm at the World Trade Center site, now known as Ground Zero. I'm holding a shovel and digging, and digging more, surrounded by a handful of firefighters doing the same thing. We are in what were once the lower levels of the buildings—an area where the subway once shuttled in and out thousands of people by the hour. We are sifting through the rubble of the remains of the buildings. It is dark—both the mood and the surroundings.

There are no more survivors to recover—only bodies and limbs, pieces of people who were torn to shreds when the buildings collapsed. There are absolutely no members of the media, no cameras. It's the firefighters and I, and among us, no small talk, no conversation. We just dig.

I had completed countless interviews with journalists, and in public, every day I worked hard to answer questions from my fellow New Yorkers no matter where they came from or who they were. On my personal time, I often reminded my wife and children how much I loved them.

Here, deep in the bowels of what came to be called "the pit," seven stories below sea level, I dug with firefighters in the rubble of the collapsed buildings. I wanted to be next to them, work with them, and let them know I would be with them through it all.

For the first time, I came across a small piece of charred remains. I felt queasy inside. I called out, "I think I found something."

Fellow searchers came to me. As they did, a siren went off and a stretcher was brought in. All work at the site stopped. Simultaneously, hundreds of workers took off their hats and placed them over their hearts.

The bones, with some remaining flesh, were retrieved. Firefighters gathered around and formed a line to help remove the remains in the most respectable way possible. The stretcher was covered with an American flag, and four men carried it slowly and respectfully up a seven-story ramp to a waiting ambulance. It was a moment I will never forget. There were many more.

When this happened the first time, I took a long pause to look at the men around me, who wore their FDNY hats and jackets with pride. Something caught my attention about them, and there's no politically correct way to say it. They were old. Some of them must have been in their seventies.

They were FDNY retirees. They were there—and this is emotional for me to write—to recover their children. *Their children.*

Many firefighter families are generational. It's that way all around the US, and New Yorkers are no exception. These were retired firefighters who had put their uniforms back on and come directly to Ground Zero after they lost communication with their kids…and eventually lost all hope.

These were fathers searching for their dead children.

They continued to dig, many working through their desperation and sadness, hoping that *maybe* they would find their child.

This moment in particular was one of the most inspirational and terribly sad moments for me after 9/11. Here were these retired firefighters coming together, determined to make peace and move on. Some would never find their children; others would dig for weeks on end, unaware of whether or not they had recovered a child. It didn't matter. They were there together. They were there as a team, bonded by a terrible tragedy and hellish circumstances that seemed to never end.

They fought through. They did the work no one else could. They were there to give closure to New York and move on with their heads held high. I learned from them; *I was inspired by them.* They pressed on, and symbolically, they helped America recover, find peace, and move forward.

Helping America move forward also meant rebuilding the very site we were standing on.

CHAPTER 10

ONE PATH WE SHALL NEVER CHOOSE, AND THAT IS THE PATH OF SURRENDER OR SUBMISSION

THE WORLD TRADE CENTER SITE HAD TO BE REBUILT; THERE WAS no question in my mind.

Weeks, even months after 9/11, I didn't know exactly how we would get there or what a new blueprint would look like, but I had no doubt that we needed to rebuild in a bigger, better, and unique way. As governor, I would do everything in my power to make it happen. In fact, the beautiful and powerful site you see today in Lower Manhattan was one of the toughest challenges I faced as governor in terms of grueling, tedious bureaucracy and years of meetings to pull people together and execute a vision.

I knew immediately that we had to strike a balance. We needed two specific elements that didn't compete, but instead complemented each other. First, we needed to build a memorial that would tell the story of September 11 and pay respect to the thousands of victims who had died there. Second, we needed to rebuild the commercial parts of Lower Manhattan in a way that would soar beyond what had existed on September 10 and would reclaim Lower Manhattan as a vibrant community.

Earlier in this book, I talked about the symbolism of keeping businesses in Manhattan. Rebuilding Ground Zero was another hugely symbolic issue. It would tell the world that New York was not backing down. We were moving onward and upward. But wow, this massive project wouldn't be easy! The mixture of emotion, politics, economics, and pure engineering challenges made the task enormous.

We'd already witnessed powerful, symbolic events that meant so much after 9/11. President Bush's throwing out the first pitch at the Yankees game. American Express's choosing to remain downtown. Even my shopping with Robert De Niro. These symbolic moments were dynamic and lasting.

Rebuilding would be more than just symbolism, though. I have always been a believer in one simple thing: to get somewhere, you need to know where you're going. For the rebuilding of Ground Zero to begin, we needed to know where we wanted to end. After 9/11, I needed a plan, one that would allow me to use the power that flowed from my position as governor to make sure Ground Zero was rebuilt appropriately and to see that all of Lower Manhattan was attended to, also rising from the ashes. I knew we needed to focus above and beyond simply where the towers had stood.

After 9/11, Rudy Giuliani and I met almost every day. He was nearing the end of his term and coming to grips with it. Both of us were campaigning for a long-shot candidate to succeed him: onetime Democrat Michael Bloomberg, who was running as a Republican. Rudy and I were anomalies as elected Republicans in New York. The city, in particular, was still very liberal. Republican candidate Bloomberg, even with the money he was spending, faced tough odds. He was squaring off against Mark Green, an ultraliberal Democrat. I was concerned about what would happen with the federal dollars I was lobbying for in Washington if Bloomberg lost and Green were elected.

With the billions in lost property and infrastructure the state was dealing with after the terror attacks, I was asking for federal assistance to help rebuild. I traveled to Washington often, meeting with the president as well as House and Senate leaders. Getting federal dollars, especially when you're asking for billions, is not easy. I had to sell legislators on the fact that this was an attack on America, not just New York City. New York is a symbol of America, and the response had to be from America. The attack destroyed so much more than the towers. Infrastructure had been wiped out—the subway, streets, electrical grid, and more were ruined.

Mid-conversation with Rudy about federal dollars, I saw him tense up. Then he let his opinion rip: "George, Mark Green is going to be mayor, and this guy is going to destroy any kind of future for Lower Manhattan."

Not only was Green the Democrats' nominee, but he had survived a brutal primary and come out strong.

"Rudy, you're probably right, and that's a problem. We can't let him have control. What do you think he'll do with Ground Zero?"

Rudy sometimes has this look when he's answering that might be serious, might be humorous, but will definitely be provocative. He purses his lips, but then the pursing ever so slightly turns into a smile. His eyes get really big. And then...

"He'll take millions of federal dollars and build a bunch of affordable housing!"

I let out a small chuckle, looked Rudy in the eyes and, nodding, responded: "It'll be a big problem. Let me take a look. I have an idea."

I didn't know it yet, but the idea I came up with would fundamentally change the direction of Lower Manhattan forever. I knew that whoever won the mayor's race, I needed to have control.

The city and state each had multiple agencies overseeing the rebuilding of Lower Manhattan. Some of these entities were eligible for federal funds, but the situation was tricky. The Democrats in control of the Senate, especially with Senators Hillary Clinton and Chuck Schumer of New York, were unlikely to allow federal dollars to flow to a Republican governor, meaning me. And with Green likely to become New York City's next mayor, he could also complicate the situation, diverting funds and shutting down any vision I wanted to execute. Furthermore, if Green were elected, the Bush administration could also hold back funds from the city. So, I came up with the idea to create a new state-city authority, called the Lower Manhattan Development Corporation, known as the LMDC. It would receive all federal funds and lead the effort to rebuild Lower Manhattan.

Rudy agreed to it. The new board of directors would have nine members. But there was a catch. The state, essentially meaning me as governor, would appoint six members. The city would get three. I wanted absolute control. Before I even knew what the vision was for a reconstructed and revitalized Lower Manhattan, I wanted to be sure I played the major part executing that vision, regardless of who took control of city hall. We put the best of the best together on the LMDC. It was headed up by John Whitehead, who'd had decades of success in the public and private sector, as well as other successful entrepreneurs and community leaders with vision and tenacity. Many also had strong, domineering personalities.

The Port Authority controlled the site and first came to us with a plan to rebuild. Its city planner drew up about four or five nondescript buildings to populate the millions of square feet. Immediately, I knew this idea wasn't appropriate. Sure, it would have been fine for a random few blocks in Midtown, but not at Ground Zero. No way. The board agreed with me.

With the LMDC under my control, I directed the group to launch what we called an innovative design study, inviting designers from around the world to submit plans to redevelop the millions of square feet destroyed in the attacks. We received more than four hundred submissions and whittled them down to seven teams of architects. Each team received a stipend of forty thousand dollars to present models and renderings of their designs.

As the entries came in, my vision became clearer. Lower Manhattan would balance two important components. First, we had to tell the story of September 11 for future generations. They needed to see, feel, and sense the magnitude of what had happened. Second, we needed to restore the economy of Lower Manhattan. A memorial and commercial revitalization would move forward hand in hand. We would show the world that we would not retreat or cave to terrorists. We would rebuild and rise beyond the Twin Towers to new heights. A thriving economy and a sacred, peaceful memorial would coexist.

Balance was key.

To say that the administration of this site was complicated would be massively understating a huge understatement. The place was an absolute mess of public and private bureaucracies intertwined, woven into each other, and literally lying on top of one another.

Ready? Here we go.

The Port Authority, which is a bi-state authority composed of an equal number of commissioners from each state, owned the land where the towers had stood. Real estate guru Larry Silverstein had the development rights. The Port Authority Trans-Hudson (PATH) controlled the railroad line that ran under and circled the entire site. The roads were run by the State of New York's Department of Transportation (DOT), unless they were the local ones owned by the city's DOT. The Metropolitan Transportation Authority (MTA) controlled the seven subway lines that ran under the site.

Each one of those entities had its own insurer. And as if all that weren't enough, the whole site went down seven stories under the roads and below sea level, to bedrock well below the waters of the Hudson River.

Did you get all that?

I had to deal with bureaucrats, technocrats, union heads, community leaders, and appointees. And both the Port Authority and PATH were bi-state agencies, meaning New Jersey had to agree to any action taken by either of them. Along with the city and state organizations, I had to talk to, placate, and make deals with local politicians and heads of corporations. Of course, I also had to win over the people—New Yorkers, millions densely packed on the island, including families who had lost loved ones—and all of them had strong opinions. Those families, understandably, were emotionally invested in every decision. Their powerful voices weighed on me heavily.

As city and state leaders and local business owners all began sharing their ideas about what they wanted to develop, there was an immediate outcry from the public. No one wanted a tourist destination, certainly not a Rockefeller Center or Times Square downtown where the towers had once stood. No one wanted something gaudy. They wanted balance, and I would make sure we met that need.

The LMDC approached these two paths—remembrance and renewal—delicately, making sure Lower Manhattan would remain economically viable while paying tribute to the victims. If businesses fled from downtown, there would be massive negative consequences for the borough, the city, and the state. Rebuilding meant restoring the economy in Lower Manhattan with commercial ventures. It also meant showing the world that America would never back down in the face of terrorism.

* * *

THE YEAR 2002 WAS EASILY ONE OF THE MOST INTENSE, STRESSFUL, amazing, and rewarding years of my life.

The challenges New York faced stretched far beyond Lower Manhattan. In the city, we were trying to prevent an economic catastrophe with companies threatening to leave. In Albany, we were dealing with an unprecedented collapse in government revenues that created a huge hole in the budget. And there was one other enormously important task I had to complete: get reelected.

I was first elected in 1994, and this would be my third term as governor. Not running was never an option. I had planned to serve only two terms. But there was absolutely no way I was going to leave office with the state in an economic downspin, Lower Manhattan in distress, and Ground Zero still smoldering. The year was grueling. It was uplifting. It was sad. It was inspirational. The days and nights blended together. My life became a montage.

Wake up at home in Garrison. "Good morning, Libby!" Say goodbye to Libby and the kids. Mornings in Albany. Travel to the city for lunch. Off to one of the boroughs for a funeral. Back to Albany for evening meetings. Home to bed in Garrison. Wife and kids are asleep. Wake up. See the family for a few minutes. Head upstate for campaign events. Whirlwind stops, east to west. Syracuse. Rochester. Buffalo. Back to the city. Sleep in the city. Meetings in the city. Return to Garrison. Wife and kids are asleep. Wake up at home. "Good morning, Libby!" Say goodbye to Libby and the kids…

Though the days and nights were long, this campaign didn't require nearly as much travel as in years past. The best way for a sitting governor to get reelected is not to campaign but to govern. I would press on, executing my vision for New York City and enacting conservative policy for the state by doing what I did best—working hard.

At night, after particularly intense days, I had to find ways to wind down and eventually get some sleep. Some people meditate; others have a drink or two. I watched mind-numbing TV.

First, I started with interesting and insightful shows on the History and Discovery channels. Anything at all irrelevant to politics was a welcome distraction. But then a terrible trend started. Political commercials kicked in. Look, I understand that commercials irritate us all, but there were two problems here. First, I was watching these channels to avoid politics, and second, these commercials were political ads attacking me!

Deep into the campaign, billionaire candidate Tom Golisano, running on the Independence Party ticket, launched ads to smear me. So, just as I was starting to wind down at night, with my eyelids slowly descending over my pupils while watching that guy with the crazy hair talk about ancient aliens, I would see my face with a narrator calling me a crook.

Ha! A crook? Really?

The attack ads didn't bother me; that's part of being elected to office. Politics did, though. All I wanted was to turn on, tune in, and drop out!

It gets better. The campaign consultant to Golisano who had convinced him to run millions of dollars' worth of ads to destroy me, while of course making millions of dollars himself, was none other than Roger Stone. Yes, *that* Roger Stone, the self-proclaimed "dirty trickster." *The* Roger Stone who was dragged out of his home in a predawn raid by more than a dozen heavily armed, flak jacket-wearing FBI agents, in connection with the Mueller Russia probe in 2019.

After a good laugh, I shut the TV off and decided that the next night I'd have to find some new station to watch that didn't air political ads.

Click. Enough Roger Stone commercials!

Go to bed. Wake up. Off to Manhattan.

In the city, I took meetings with heads of city and state agencies; others were with owners of mom-and-pop shops. Every one of those businesses was critical in rebuilding the community of Lower Manhattan. While large corporations like American Express symbolically stood out for the world to see, the smaller businesses glued everything together. From dry-cleaning businesses, to delis and restaurants, to convenience stores, these mom-and-pop shops were used and visited every day by the thousands of people working downtown.

These business owners legitimately feared that the city and their livelihoods would never recover. I took meetings with people while traces of smoke still emanated from the rubble. Understandably, they were despondent and hopeless, and they let me know.

"Sir, something needs to be done now, right now! We're never going to make it!"

"Governor, when will the subway start running again?"

"Mr. Pataki, how about the debris? Can we start by getting that cleared out...now?"

I learned early on when I was mayor of Peekskill that giving out specific dates is a problem. You do everything you can as a leader to lead, push projects through, and hold people accountable, but oftentimes people miss deadlines, costs exceed budget, or some contracted companies simply fail. But now, after 9/11, I not only gave people specific dates, I worked to give them hope by conveying our sense of urgency. Under my watch, no one floundered about or was idle. It was all hands on deck to get the city back up and running.

Shortly after 9/11, small groups of people and businesses began to band together. It was an amazing phenomenon. At first, many of the downtown businesses formed support groups. Some were in the same industry. Others were in different industries but were friendly because they were located nearby. They teamed up and joined hands in a way similar to that of political grassroots organizations. It didn't matter if they had once competed—they banded together, becoming support centers for one another. Soon after, the groups shifted into advocating for the area, working with me to push for funding for specific projects and redevelopment of certain areas.

The groups were diverse, ranging from businesses owners to art lovers. People funneled their anger and frustration into advocating and creating. New Yorkers were helping New Yorkers. It was beautiful.

Some celebrities, who knew they could command attention and do good work, also stepped up. Sigourney Weaver teamed with big developers; the group became an advocate for the area, pushing for and eventually creating new parks and festivals. Sure enough, Robert De Niro entered the picture again. As I worked with business owners on incentive packages and tax breaks, trying to restore their faith, De Niro and prolific film producer Jane Rosenthal announced the Tribeca Film Festival. They began the festival in Lower Manhattan in direct response to the attacks. It was another powerful symbol of resilience in the face of devastation. These people cared about the city, and they were determined to rebuild and revitalize it.

One neighborhood that faced a huge uphill battle was Battery Park City, which sat directly west of the site of the former World Trade Center towers, across the street. It was utterly devastated in the wake of the attacks.

Before 9/11, most of downtown was a place where people went to work and then left. Battery Park City was one of the few neighborhoods in the area that had just started to develop. Under my predecessor, Governor Cuomo, redevelopment languished. When I took office in the mid-'90s, we got the area going again. New residential towers got built; thousands of people were moving in. Located on the Hudson River on the lower west side of the island, Battery Park City was a beautiful spot with huge potential.

When 9/11 hit, power, plumbing, and the subway got wiped out. Large, identifiable piles of debris littered the neighborhood, including pieces of luggage from the hijacked planes and emergency vehicles destroyed by the towers as they crashed down and shot outward. Thick ash covered everything like a fresh snowfall. Significant parts of the buildings themselves, those closest to the towers, had been damaged directly.

Weeks after the attacks, as the cleanup progressed, some residents held out hope that they'd be able to move back in. But no matter how intensely the cleanup crews worked, dust and ash remained everywhere. Tenants left. Some buildings had 0 percent occupancy.

In the '90s, as Battery Park City was being developed, a few companies expressed interest in moving there. The prestigious powerhouse investment bank Goldman Sachs was one of them. This would be huge for the up-and-coming area.

Goldman had buildings scattered throughout parts of Manhattan. By 2001, company higher-ups were considering consolidating their business into one large world headquarters smack in the middle of the area. The plan was to build a forty-something-story building at 200 West Street in Battery Park City, just between Murray and Vesey Streets.

It was one thing to keep a company like American Express in Lower Manhattan, but this was something entirely different. Amex was recommitting by staying; Goldman was a global giant with a *new* pledge to build its new world headquarters in a tower across the street from Ground Zero, investing billions of dollars—which would bring a brand-new development and a fresh injection of confidence and much-needed capital.

Goldman was as critical to the redevelopment of downtown as any major corporation. With employees spread out around the city, its headquarters would bring nearly ten thousand workers together in one large building.

This was a huge opportunity for all of New York City and the state. It was one of the seeds that grew and shaped downtown into what it is today—a spectacular neighborhood where people live, work, and play. I knew with the right kind of inspiration and planning we could bring downtown to life. The Goldman headquarters, along with other, smaller start-up businesses, and celebrities bringing cultural events to the area would be the start of it all.

So many people working downtown creates an opportunity for developers to build residential places for those employees to live. When people move in, so do restaurants, bars, shops, and a whole lot more. Everything was connected, and Goldman would play a big part in bringing a huge number of people to downtown, anchored in one spot. If Goldman bailed and chose a different site, it would have been a big blow to the city. As with American Express, it was critical for Goldman to commit, especially in this area.

As I dealt with city and state executives, my chief of staff, John Cahill, worked with Goldman. Henry Paulson, who would eventually become secretary of the treasury under George W. Bush, was heading up the company at that time. John was on the phone with the Goldman people almost every day, trying to allay concerns and fears. And there were plenty. While I was dealing with all of the economic challenges statewide, John became the point person for Lower Manhattan.

After long days and nights of meetings in the city, I'd head back to Garrison to sleep at home, but with a different set of TV viewing habits. Now, months into the campaign of 2002, I had the pleasure of watching some seriously mind-numbing stuff: HGTV, Home and Garden Television. I learned about renovating kitchens and bathrooms. I also learned how to create some seriously good feng shui in my home. No "Pataki is a crook" ads here!

But sure enough, just as I started to wind down at night, with my eyelids slowly descending over my pupils, there I was—my face with a narrator calling me a crook.

Ha! Not here, while I'm learning that a wind chime can help strengthen the qi *of an area!*

Who convinced Golisano to run political ads on HGTV? Roger Stone, of course.

Click.

Go to bed. Wake up. Off to Albany.

Work in the capital was especially tough. Our budget team worked day and night to try to keep the finances of the state together. After 9/11, the state's coffers took a nosedive. As less and less revenue came in, expenses went up. It was a nightmare finding our way through that, facing billions of dollars in deficits. The numbers had not been this bad since the Great Depression. And the decline in revenues continued for three straight years. Hundreds of thousands of private-sector jobs were lost as the economy dropped, seemingly with no bottom. At the same time, we were looking at losing major companies and trying to figure out how to rebuild.

After long days and nights in Albany, I returned home. This time, though, I had a radically different plan for TV. I chose stations that I was certain wouldn't have any commercials about that "crook" Pataki. I'd had enough of that guy! So, I started watching Univision and Telemundo. It worked out well because I was trying to improve my Spanish anyway. A massive part of our campaign was devoted to Latino outreach. And spoiler alert: it paid off in the end.

Just as *las noticias* (the news) was finishing and I was starting to wind down, with my eyelids slowly descending over my pupils, the anchor finished up the news, and there I was again—my face with a narrator calling me a *ladron*, Spanish for…you guessed it: crook!

Eres un pendejo, Roger Stone!

Click.

Go to bed. Wake up. Off to win an election!

After an exhausting, exhilarating, and inspirational ten months, November 5, 2002, Election Day, rolled around. We won, and won big.

Drained but motivated by the faith put in me, and knowing we had such monumental tasks ahead, I addressed supporters that night with an emotional speech.

> *There are no stronger, better people than New Yorkers. And when we are united, when we stand together, we can accomplish miracles. And it's been my goal as governor not to be the governor of some, but to be the governor of all.*

We beat the Democratic nominee, Carl McCall, by such a huge percentage that *The New York Times* noted that McCall "came dangerously close last night to making history in another way, as the Democratic candidate who received the smallest percentage of total votes in modern history for a statewide race." As for Tom Golisano, he ended up spending seventy-four million dollars of his own money to come in a distant third. And as a Republican, my broken Spanish helped me to actually win the Latino vote. Gracias, Señor Stone.

The reelection was a reaffirmation. It cemented the fact that New Yorkers put their faith in me to execute a vision for the state and the city, including the rebuilding of the city, and more specifically, *how* we would rebuild the city. More confident than ever, I was ready to continue advancing my vision.

I took a few days to spend time with my family after the election, knowing another four years of tough work were on the horizon. Before bed, I still unwound with a little television. This time I flipped the channels freely, without seeing even one mention of that "crook" George Pataki.

Go to bed. Wake up. Off to Manhattan.

* * *

By February 2003, the LMDC had decided on two finalists for the Ground Zero Master Site Plan—Rafael Viñoly and Daniel Libeskind—announced them in a press conference, and set a date for later that month to have them present their final plans to the board. Then we would vote.

Viñoly was a Uruguay-born architect with offices in New York, Argentina, and other parts of the world. He had put together an international team of architects, a group that branded themselves THINK. The other architect, Libeskind, was an immigrant to the United States from Poland and the son of Holocaust survivors.

Before we get into the decision-making process, I want to share something with you: my mind was made up. I'd already settled on the best plan. I didn't reveal my preferred plan publicly, though. I wanted the process to play out without my influence. However, there was no doubt in my mind which design was the perfect fit.

After months of exhaustive efforts, the LMDC was ready to vote and officially name the winning architect. The decision didn't come easily. The morning of decision day was an absolute slap in the face. I was blindsided. Waking up at home in Garrison with my family, the phone rang. It was my longtime friend Eddie Hayes.

"Hello?"

"Well, I guess we didn't win!"

And good morning to you, too! I thought.

Eddie was a prominent New York lawyer who was representing Daniel Libeskind in the site's competition. Clearly, he was upset.

"What?" I asked.

"We're out! Didn't you see the *Times*?"

"Out? What do you mean, Eddie?"

As I asked, I dumped *The New York Times* out of its plastic bag and onto my kitchen table. With the phone pressed to my ear with my shoulder, I opened the paper and saw it. The headline read, "Panel Supports 2 Tall Towers At Disaster Site." The article paraphrased an anonymous, zealously overconfident committee member. It said the committee had recommended Viñoly's plan and—incredibly—stated that "several committee members believe that the mayor and the governor should pay heed to their preference." By this time, Michael Bloomberg, the underdog in his election, had been serving as mayor for more than a year and inherited Rudy's seat on the LMDC board. That anonymous board member was then quoted as saying, "We don't expect anyone to overrule us." *Ha!* Told you we appointed some strong, domineering personalities.

"Eddie," I said in a frustrated tone. "Eddie, I'll see you at the meeting today. I'm calling Mike now."

With the paper sprawled out in front of me, I hung up and called Mayor Bloomberg. During his short time serving, we had established a solid rapport.

"Hello."

"Mike?"

"Yes, George?"

"Yeah. Hey, have you seen the *Times* today?"

"I did."

"So, you saw the article. Do you agree with this decision the board seems to have made, picking Viñoly?"

"Well, I haven't looked at the plans that closely, but I certainly haven't made a decision."

"I think the Viñoly plan is awful. I love the Libeskind ideas, though, and we really need to get this right. I'll see you downtown."

Though I was a big fan of the Libeskind design and knew it was best for the city, I created the public process to get people involved as much as possible, confident it would make clear what I knew: the Libeskind plan was the one. But after seeing this article, I knew there was going to be a fight, and one I needed to win.

I got off the phone and went to Manhattan, where I met John Cahill at my Midtown office. From there, we hopped in a car and headed south, downtown to the LMDC offices, which actually overlooked the wreckage at Ground Zero. As we drove, I looked up at the sky. Months before, smoke had stopped rising from the ashes of the attacks, but it was still a relief to look at a clear sky. Gazing out the window, I visualized both the Viñoly and Libeskind plans. I pictured how their visions—radically different from each other—would look hovering over Manhattan.

Cahill and I pulled up to the meeting location downtown and hopped out of the car. I took in a deep breath of the cold February air, paused, and took a look around—and up—knowing that the decision we were about to make would change the New York City skyline forever. This was something I did not take lightly. I had studied both plans intensely, getting to know the ins and outs of each one, from where the memorial would be placed to the function of each and every building that would potentially replace the towers. I knew both plans so well that I was planning to go into the meeting and ask rhetorical questions to shine a light on certain shortcomings and strengths.

We got inside, where members of the board were greeting one another with the usual pleasantries. I saw Mayor Bloomberg and walked directly over to him.

"Mike."

"George."

We shook hands and sat next to each other in the middle of the panel.

There was no guarantee how this would play out. While Mike and I had appointed LMDC members, they were independent and certainly had the right to reject my wishes. I also had no idea which direction Mike would go in.

Viñoly's THINK team presented first. From the start, the board members could clearly see they weren't on their A game. The architects commented how they had just flown in from Buenos Aires the night before. Let's face it: *they flew in at the last minute because they thought they had it in the bag.* I know for certain that someone on the board had told them they won even before that article went to print in the *Times*. The THINK team was overconfident, and their lackluster presentation reflected it. As they displayed their renderings and models, the presenters lacked energy and, quite frankly, seemed ambivalent to it all.

The Viñoly plan replicated the framework of the Twin Towers, made up of steel latticework and hollow inside.

I thought to myself pessimistically and sarcastically, *We're replicating the iconic Twin Towers with two soaring skeletons instead of anything even remotely inspiring. These things will only remind us of that day's unnerving horror.*

They were disturbing, sad, and lacked any semblance of inspiration or power. Even more disturbing, and again illustrating Viñoly's lack of awareness with this project, in an earlier version his team had placed a connecting structure on top of the two skeleton-like frames. It resembled a plane crashing into the World Trade Center. It was awful. They eventually removed that part of it.

Viñoly's team finished, and the board started asking questions. Most were irrelevant questions about Viñoly himself, not about the project, like, "What inspired you?"

I quickly grew tired of the polite conversation and weak questions. I knew the plan was loaded with flaws, so I fired off a series of quick questions.

"Do you have any idea of cost?"

"No."

"Have you or anyone else ever built anything like this?"

"No."

"Will this design enable us to rebuild ten million square feet of office space?"

"Not sure."

"Can we tour the site and get an understanding of where the towers stood?"

"No."

I abruptly stopped. Point made.

Then the mayor started. Michael Bloomberg is a blunt and to-the-point kind of guy, so much so that he directly asked Viñoly a question that some might not even think to ask, especially of an accomplished architect.

"Can you build this type of structure?"

The answer from this renowned group of architects, one of two finalists tasked with coming up with the idea to rebuild Ground Zero, should have been an unqualified yes. Instead, they answered the mayor timidly.

"We believe so."

You believe so? Not exactly reassuring.

Viñoly and his team left the room. With the team gone, the mayor leaned over to me. "George, where are you on this?"

"I don't think the Viñoly plan works or fits in any way, Mike. Let's hear out Daniel Libeskind."

The room quieted down as a smiling Daniel Libeskind walked in. He began his presentation. From the second he began speaking, it reaffirmed everything I knew in my heart of hearts. His presentation was as amazing as his renderings. Passionate and full of life, he shared his personal journey as an immigrant to America as a young boy.

"I came to the United States with my parents on a boat called the SS *Constitution*."

He added how much his parents, Holocaust survivors from Poland, loved America. His uniquely American attitude and

(Above) *Here, I'm leaving Ground Zero on the night of September 11th. At my feet, you can see a mix of shredded papers from offices in the World Trade Center towers, parts of buildings, and the thick ash that covered Lower Manhattan.*

(Left) *In a spontaneous visit, we visited a Lower Manhattan church where I'm embracing a fellow New Yorker. Whether or not you lost someone that day, it was reassuring and comforting to hug someone, knowing we were all there for each other.*

Photo by Eric Draper

September 14, 2001. Aboard Marine One, we fly over Lower Manhattan, where I update President Bush on the situation. Through the window, you can see the smoke rising from the ashes of Ground Zero.

Photo by Eric Draper

September 14, 2001. On the right, I listen as President Bush speaks into the bullhorn delivering the now historical words, "the people who knocked these buildings down will hear all of us soon."

(Left) *September 14, 2001. The President, Mayor Giuliani, and I embrace on the tarmac of McGuire Air Force Base. It was the first time the Mayor and I had seen the President since the attack.*

(Below) *September 20, 2001, 10:40 a.m. This picture illustrates the catastrophic damage caused when the North and South World Trade Center Towers fell. Behind me, you see the skeleton of the North Tower. Below that is what was left of the Marriott Hotel, which was twenty-two stories.*

October 14, 2001. Here, I proudly walk with New York's finest, bravest heroes. We are walking north on Greenwich Street near Warren Street. Behind us, smoke still rises from Ground Zero.

(Above) *April 2002. After spending the afternoon digging with firefighters through the rubble, I was asked to lead a procession for remains recovered that day. Firefighters covered the remains in an American flag and walked them up from the lower levels of the World Trade Center.*

(Right) *April 2002. In this heartbreaking photo, I stand beside a retired New York City firefighter. He was one of the many retirees and fathers who came to Ground Zero to dig through the rubble and search for his child lost in the wreckage.*

In Albany, I finish addressing members of the state legislature, where I worked with Democrats and Republicans to straighten out the financial disaster after 9/11 and get New York's economy back on track.

This is the reveal of the final model of the Freedom Tower, complete with the security-based changes.

Here, as I point to the Freedom Tower, I smile proudly looking at the master plan model. From left to right, you see the head of the Empire State Development Corporation, Charlie Gargano, David Childs, the architect of the Freedom Tower, myself, and Daniel Libeskind, the visionary of the master plan.

I look at the Freedom Tower today the same way I did shortly after it was completed—with tremendous pride. It hovers over the magnificent skyline of New York City and rises higher than any other building in North America, celebrating our triumphant recovery after the attacks.

energy—as an immigrant and a patriot—was intertwined with and embedded in his presentation and, ultimately, his designs. His personal story, his vision, and the design itself captured the spirit of America.

Libeskind's plan was to build the main building, the Freedom Tower, 1,776 feet tall, paying homage to the year America was founded. It also meant the structure would rise higher than the World Trade Center towers.

He continued his energetic and passionate presentation, bringing in illustrations from all angles. He displayed imagery of the Brooklyn Bridge on one side coming into Manhattan, connecting the boroughs, connecting the people, and connecting dreams. On the other side, the Freedom Tower stood tall, with the buildings next to it aligned in descending order, in remembrance of those who had died. He incorporated an area for a museum, and he left an open space for a memorial exactly where the towers once stood.

Libeskind went the extra mile by identifying a wall that was buried underground, invisible to the public. It's referred to as the slurry wall, as in a concrete slurry. The wall surrounded what was called "the bathtub," but that's a misnomer. The walls of this "bathtub" were meant to keep water from the Hudson River out of the foundation of the World Trade Center. Libeskind made the wall a central component, saying, "It stands for the indomitable spirit of New York and as a miracle of engineering as well."

Had that slurry wall broken, it would have flooded seven stories with raging Hudson River water. Thousands more people could have been killed. With all the carnage that day, somehow the slurry had stood strong, saving countless lives.

His design showed that America stood tall in the face of terror, while honoring the more than 2,500 people who had died there. It was exactly what Lower Manhattan needed. It was what the country needed.

Libeskind wrapped up his presentation by saying this was "about paying homage to the great heroes and also about seeing the city move forward." Daniel Libeskind knew precisely what I and so many other New Yorkers wanted for Ground Zero: *balance*. We would rebuild *and* we would honor the dead.

Libeskind left the room. The board members were visibly impressed, but I wasn't sure they were convinced. Reflecting on the gossip and anonymous quotes in *The New York Times* article about paying "heed to their preference," I got right to the point: "I take it you are all in favor of Viñoly."

A few nodded. Others, who saw my concern with the Viñoly presentation and design, hedged, not really answering. I came right out and said it: "You're not going to build those skeletons."

A few jaws dropped.

Bloomberg was as frustrated as I was. He then referred to the Viñoly plan and said something I couldn't believe: "They look like the Elmhurst gas tanks I just paid millions to have removed."

I clenched my jaw to stop from laughing out loud; I couldn't help but smile. This offhand, hilarious quip was highly revealing. The Elmhurst tanks, as they were known, had made for both an eyesore and a landmark. The two-hundred-foot-tall skeletal remains that once housed gas tanks had stood next to the Long Island Expressway. Local traffic reporters had used them to identify just how backed up traffic into Manhattan was. In other words, they were ugly, and the only time people thought about them was when they were angry as hell that traffic into the city was backed up.

While I let the process work itself out for months, it was clear that the board was going in the wrong direction. I knew that if they picked the wrong design, I would be the one held responsible, and rightfully so. If this was going to be my thing, *it was going to be my thing*. The Libeskind proposal was the most appropriate and inspirational. It was the right fit for Manhattan, representing the resilience of our city and our country while maintaining the sanctity of the area.

The board clearly saw what I wanted. That, coupled with Viño-ly's slightly disturbing design and Bloomberg's strong support and gas-tank comments, sealed the deal. The votes were in. The board members, including those who had originally supported Viñoly, voted for the right plan. Libeskind won. The board basically said, "You're the governor. He's the mayor. We'll vote for your plan."

Cahill and I walked out of the meeting. We stayed silent in the elevator ride down. Then we stepped outside. Returning to the cold, brisk air, I paused for a brief moment and did a 360, looking at the skyline, or at least what was left of it. Confident and content, I nodded and smiled.

"Governor."

"Yeah, John," I answered, still looking up at the skyline.

"That went really well."

"I know, and I'm really happy with the outcome."

"Sir."

John paused to lead into something larger. "Sir, you know the work has just begun, though, right?"

Still looking up, I nodded, and then looked over at him at my side. "Yes, it has. Now we have to build it."

He raised an eyebrow and said, "Yep, but we still have Goldman."

"Goldman Sachs," I whispered to myself, still nodding, reflecting on the successful meeting.

Leaving that meeting with the right plan for downtown was invigorating. The momentum was energizing. We were going to rebuild Lower Manhattan in a big, bold way. But John was right. A new set of headaches had just begun.

The remaining challenges included more than just rebuilding Ground Zero. After the Libeskind plan was picked, our focus broadened to rebuilding large portions of Lower Manhattan.

Goldman Sachs and the NYPD would be major parts of that. Neither would be easy to work with.

* * *

ON SUNDAY, JULY 4, 2004, WE LAID THE FIRST CORNERSTONE AT the World Trade Center.

In an emotional and powerful moment, I addressed the crowd.

The terrorists who attacked us hoped to break our spirit, but instead they broke our hearts. How badly they underestimated the resiliency of this city and the resolve of these United States. In less than three years, we have more than just plans on paper—we place here today the cornerstone, the foundation of a new tower.

With a bagpipe procession playing "God Bless America," a twenty-ton slab of granite was laid, marking the start of construction on the 1,776-foot Freedom Tower. It is inscribed, "To honor and remember those who lost their lives on September 11, 2001, and as a tribute to the enduring spirit of freedom—July Fourth 2004."

All of the key city, state, and political players attended, including Mayor Bloomberg and the New York Police Department. I mention the NYPD because if we thought we had challenges before, the NYPD was about to make the construction of the Freedom Tower significantly more difficult.

Months after the cornerstone was laid, Cahill briefly mentioned to me that the NYPD had "some concerns" about the location of the Freedom Tower. With his active role in rebuilding Lower Manhattan, he was getting dozens of calls and emails every day. Some were directly from top administrators; other times, he'd get fed hearsay. Now Cahill was specifically hearing that the NYPD had "security issues" with the building.

Busy governing the state, I gave John a call from Albany.

"John, what's going on?"

By this time, the NYPD had made its concerns formal and public. They had sent a formal letter to the LMDC and it had somehow leaked to the press.

"Governor, Commissioner Kelly has two issues: First, they want the Freedom Tower moved farther back from West Street. They're saying it's too close to the road, making it an easy target to strike.

And Governor, you're not going to believe this. They want it built to foreign-embassy standards."

"Foreign-embassy standards?" I asked rhetorically. No commercial building in the United States had ever been required to meet this kind of standard before, as far as I know.

I knew what he meant; I just couldn't believe the demand. When embassies are built abroad, they're built with extraordinary caution. They remain distant from roads and are built with massive, protective concrete barriers and walls to mitigate the impact of vehicle bombs and improvised explosive devices (IEDs). Already, we'd designed all sorts of security precautions for the building and everything else around it. The kinds of changes the NYPD wanted would require millions, perhaps billions more dollars to make happen.

"Okay, understood. But John, why are they making these demands now, *almost two years after the Libeskind plan got approved*? NYPD was right there at the ceremony, laying the first cornerstone with us! Construction is already underway!"

John didn't have answers, because the NYPD didn't either. There had never been a peep about security concerns until now. The NYPD blindsided us.

Remember, the Port Authority owns all of this land. It has its own set of law enforcement, but as we saw on 9/11 and in other large-scale incidents before, the NYPD often comes in as support. Now it was demanding to have a say. John and I made a trip to meet with a large group that included city and state leaders, the Port Authority, and the NYPD.

As I was listening to concerns and answering questions, the meeting started to get a little rowdy. A major concern for the NYPD and the Port Authority was safety, and people were passionate about it. I empathized but remained stone-faced and quiet.

The discussions got heated. Agency leaders started talking over one another. Decorum got thrown out; rank and positions of authority didn't matter. Making matters worse, many of these people didn't know who was who, even though the agencies worked so closely together. Many of the heads of these organizations were relatively new. On the NYPD side, the fresh faces were new Mayor Bloomberg appointees. But in the Port Authority, an entire layer of leadership had disappeared. Scores of men and women had worked at the Port Authority all their lives and now were gone. An entire generation with deep institutional knowledge just wasn't around.

They were dead—killed in the attacks.

It was yet another horrifying reminder of how the effects of 9/11 lingered and directly impacted everything we were trying to accomplish. Often the reminders came in the most mundane tasks—calling someone to ask for a meeting or sending an email to the head of an agency to notify the person about a change of plans. It was difficult to keep track of who was doing what, even for the men and women in the agencies themselves.

The frustration at the meeting peaked as NYPD members voiced their concerns about terrorism, attempted bombings, and shootings. A few started raising their voices.

"How are we gonna protect the city?"

"You know, Governor, there are some real concerns here!"

The NYPD members laid out their two main concerns: again, the location of the Freedom Tower and the construction of the building itself. They feared that busy West Street was too close, making it easy for a car packed with explosives to reach the building. They wanted it moved back sixty feet away from the road. This would require some intense redesigning by the architect, and of course, anytime you change plans, it means spending more money. They also were demanding that we build to foreign-embassy standards, meaning the Freedom Tower would be fortified to withstand bombs, enormous ones at that. The building would now have to stand on top of a two-hundred-foot concrete and steel pedestal.

As we hashed out these concerns in the meeting, the room got rowdier.

"This is a prime target for Al-Qaeda!"

"Why do we even need something so big?"

Then one of the officers yelled something I couldn't believe: "Build it in Boston!"

Wow.

Build. It. In. Boston.

The room went silent.

It was heartbreaking to hear; I understood, though. Years after 9/11, people were still genuinely frustrated, angry, and of course, scared. I looked around the silent room. All eyes turned to me. Gently nodding, I broke the silence by speaking in a quiet, firm voice.

"We'll get it done. You want it sixty feet back? We'll move it back. You want it built to embassy standards? We'll build it to embassy standards."

Everyone was stunned. They had tried to kill the building. I wasn't about to let them.

* * *

FEARS AND FRUSTRATIONS UNFOLDED IN ANOTHER GROUP AS WELL: Goldman Sachs.

Cahill and I were asked to take a meeting with Goldman's lawyers and executives. They wanted to address the fact that we were putting part of West Street underground as a tunnel. Months before, some executives had said they had issues with the tunnel's being in front of the complex.

Before we get to the over-the-top presentation by Goldman's lawyers, allow me to say this: it's my opinion that Goldman executives didn't want the tunnel because it took away from the prestige factor of rolling up to Goldman Sachs's brand-new world headquarters on West Street itself. They couldn't have the prestigious Goldman Sachs entrance sitting next to a tunnel.

In the meeting, they presented their overall concerns. After going through a PowerPoint presentation and some mundane details, they got to the tunnel. They explained that a tunnel would amplify the impact of any kind of nearby explosion—for example, an attack on the Freedom Tower.

"Now watch this," a Goldman Sachs representative said, his voice quavering. Neither John nor I had any idea what was coming next.

He hit Play on the DVD player, and a short film started. It showed a car, packed with thousands of pounds of explosives, *exploding*.

Boom!

After it blew up, there was nothing left, not even the frame of the car, only a massive crater in the ground. Cahill leaned over and whisper-shouted to me, "What the…?"

It was insensitive. It was shocking. Goldman reps made their point, quite overdramatically. Then they threatened to leave Lower Manhattan altogether. After our meeting, their threats played out in the media, where they announced they'd dropped their plans and were looking for space in Midtown.

From watching car bombs rip through tunnels to hearing, "Build it in Boston," I became only more resolute. As talks progressed among the NYPD, the Port Authority, and now Goldman, I began pushing my team, as well as state and city officials, harder. I must have repeated "just get it done" a thousand times. I knew the best thing to do was to remain focused, rely on my team, and just keep pushing.

We moved the Freedom Tower back from West Street. We redesigned the building to meet foreign-embassy standards. The tunnel where we had been shown car bombs blowing up never went underground—and keeping West Street aboveground ended up saving us hundreds of millions of dollars while allaying Goldman's fears. Our team pulled it off. After they began building their headquarters across the street from Ground Zero, Henry Paulson gave me a call. I'll never forget his words: "I thought I was tenacious. You make me look tame."

The last decision we had left for Ground Zero was to finalize the design for a memorial. Remembering those who had died and recognizing the courage of the responders was critical. To accomplish this, I again decided on a public process. We established a jury, and I picked leading experts such as Maya Lin, who had designed the Vietnam Veterans Memorial in Washington, DC.

We asked for submissions online, and the response was astounding. More than five thousand people from sixty-three nations submitted their plans. People from all over the world, regardless of their country, religion, or background, participated. It became the largest design competition in history, receiving tens of millions of clicks and comments. In the following months, the jury whittled the submissions down to a final handful.

I felt that the memorial had to do a number of things. First, I did not want any kind of building on the footprint where the two towers themselves once stood. I promised this to the family members who had lost loved ones. I also wanted visitors to understand the magnitude of our loss. The towers had been enormous. We needed to impress this upon young visitors from a future generation. Next, the memorial needed to have space underground to tell the individual stories of those who had responded and lost their lives on that awful day. It also needed to leave the slurry wall exposed and provide space to hold the numerous artifacts preserved after the attack. Finally, aboveground, we wanted to list the name of every single person who died in the attacks, while having a peaceful, natural space in the middle of chaotic downtown to give visitors a chance to reflect.

As we neared the end of the selection process, I sat down with Michael Arad, a young, unknown architect who worked for the New York City Department of Housing. He had created an amazing design that I thought fit perfectly. He called it *Reflecting Absence.*

Arad designed the memorial with voids where the towers had stood. Each void held a waterfall, gently falling into a reflecting pool at the bottom. Around the sides of the two voids, the names of all the people who had died would be engraved so that family members and others could visit and pay their respects. Arad's plan achieved all that I had hoped. The voids where the towers had stood revealed their magnitude. The waterfalls and reflecting pool brought respectful silence to the thousands of names carved around them. And the underground space was perfect for the Memorial Museum to hold the artifacts. Lending a hand, noted landscape architect Peter Walker joined the project to arrange trees and plants around the plaza to provide the tranquil, peaceful mood we desired.

The plan was done and submitted. Mayor Bloomberg and I submitted our thoughts, and the jury made its selection. Unlike the battle over the Master Site Plan, this time things went smoothly. The jury made the obvious and correct choice, *Reflecting Absence*. I was thrilled.

Now all of the components were set, including the Master Site Plan, the Freedom Tower, and the memorial. You have to appreciate the years and years of work behind this. We picked Libeskind's site plan in February 2003. We didn't pick the memorial designer until 2004. And the final plans to satisfy the NYPD and Goldman didn't materialize until 2005.

In those years, which flew by, Cahill dealt mostly with the rebuilding of Ground Zero and Goldman Sachs. Meanwhile, another good friend, Charlie Gargano, dealt with thousands of other existing businesses downtown. He worked around the clock to lure businesses to New York. Charlie is soft-spoken but firm, to-the-point but charming. The debonair, always impeccably dressed Charlie has perfectly blown-out silver hair. Charlie not only looks like he's straight out of Central Casting in Hollywood, but he's played some small parts in movies, including *Serendipity* and, appropriately enough, *World Trade Center*. Aside from his hobby as an actor, Charlie has had decades of success in the public and private sectors. He was the vice chair of the Port Authority. The bistate organization always has someone from New Jersey as chair, and a New Yorker gets the vice-chair slot. On top of that, Charlie headed up the statewide economic development team known as the Empire State Development Corporation, or ESDC. The organization deals with the business community, providing support or pushing for legislative changes on behalf of industries and employers. It also works hard to help small- and medium-sized companies grow, while reaching out around the globe to encourage companies to come to New York.

Charlie was a key person assisting the Lower Manhattan Development Corporation. The LMDC was brand new, so it didn't have an economic development arm; the ESDC administered all of the funds to the LMDC. Charlie, with his experience and expertise, directed the economic programs and oversaw every penny. And to this day, I'm proud to say that every single dollar of the twenty billion dollars was accounted for—no missing funds, no ridiculous or egregious expenditures.

Regardless of the exhaustive years of work we put in and all the time that had passed, I was as determined as ever. I had a crystal-clear vision for Ground Zero. That vision would be executed.

Something else in my life became clear at this time. On July 27, 2005, in Albany, I announced I would not seek a fourth term as governor:

> Together we have changed the fundamental direction of this state to one that powers the individual and not the government. New York is a different state, a better state than it was ten years ago. We've done a lot together, and yet there is always more to do. But there's one thing I've understood from my very first day in public office: that as elected officials we are only temporary stewards of the people's trust. So today with pride in our accomplishments, enduring enthusiasm for New York's future, and heartfelt gratitude to its people, I am announcing that I will not seek another term as your governor.

The state spent a few years recovering from mismanagement prior to my first term and later the 9/11 attacks. By 2005, New York was making a strong comeback. Jobs were growing, revenue was increasing, and deficits once again had been turned into surpluses. The only reason for me to run for a fourth term would have been ego. I wanted to leave on a high note.

With the economy doing well, the state recovering, and the Freedom Tower on track to revive, rebuild, and reenergize Lower Manhattan, I was confident this was the right time to go. Plus, without a fourth term, I wouldn't have to deal with another campaign. I could focus on what was important for the state and step down with grace, proud of my accomplishments.

Two final challenges remained that could have prevented the Freedom Tower from getting built: time and Eliot Spitzer. In 2006, Spitzer clinched the Democratic nomination for governor and was the favorite to take office.

My decision to not seek a fourth term left me until January 2007 to get everything done. It was a race against time, but I knew that with the help of my staff, and Cahill in particular, we could push to have steel in the ground before I left office.

After battling all the pushback, we wanted to make sure nothing else would stop the Freedom Tower from being built. There was only one possible barrier—a change in politics. We absolutely, unquestionably had to insulate the Freedom Tower from the shifting political winds, which can turn quickly in New York.

Throughout 2006, city leaders and the eventual governor-elect himself, Eliot Spitzer, stated their concerns to the press about the Freedom Tower. Even greedy competing developers, who wanted to launch their own projects or feared competition, aired their grievances in full-page ads saying not to build the Freedom Tower, claiming they knew what was best for the security of downtown.

The press ate it up. A *New York Times* article quoted civic leaders and real-estate executives as saying the Freedom Tower was "too big" and would be "unlikely to attract corporate tenants." Repeatedly, the *Times* quoted Spitzer as saying he had concerns it could turn into "a white elephant." Spitzer's staff said as soon as they took office, they would immediately put the Freedom Tower plans "under review."

To me, along with the memorial, the Freedom Tower was the essential element of Libeskind's entire plan. Yes, we would rebuild and remember, but we would also celebrate our freedom in an enthusiastic, open, and typically American way. We would rise beyond where the Twin Towers had stood on September 11.

Cahill and I would read these articles and pick the phone up first thing in the morning to talk.

"John, we have to get the structure started. We need steel in the ground, and we need it in before January."

In January 2007, Spitzer would be sworn in, and the way I saw it was that if steel structures had already been erected, it would be highly unlikely that his administration would go in, remove them, and stop the project. Politically, it would reflect horribly on the new governor. Public outrage would never let it happen.

In November 2006, a major portion of concrete was poured onto the foundation. In December, the public was invited to sign a thirty-foot steel beam, which went into the ground two days later. Then, in January, eight days after Governor Spitzer was sworn in, a second set of beams was placed on top of the first.

As Spitzer was taking office, his staff *still* pushed back, saying the design was "under review." But businesses were snatching up leases all over Lower Manhattan, and vacancy rates were dropping fast. The revival of Lower Manhattan was happening.

On the cold winter morning of Monday, February 13, 2007, I woke up at my home in Garrison. Now, as *former* Governor Pataki, it was such a pleasure to start the day in my peaceful, serene, and warm home with my kids and my wife, Libby. For this brief moment in my life, I had nowhere to go and nothing to do. I put on some clothes and shoes and strolled outside to grab the newspaper on the driveway. Back in the house, I poured a cup of coffee and sat down to read *The New York Times*. The headline read, "Spitzer, in Reversal, Is Expected to Approve Freedom Tower, Officials Say."

The Freedom Tower would be built.

I set the paper down on the table, sipped my coffee, and just stared at the headline for a few minutes, smiling.

There were naysayers. There were people with business interests. There were people with legitimate, well-intentioned concerns about the site's security. And undoubtedly, there were people living in fear. On September 12, 2001, I knew we had to overcome. We would not be intimidated. We would not surrender. Like the mythological phoenix, we would rise again.

Still today, when I arrive at or leave my office in Midtown, I take a moment to gaze at the skyline. I'm proud of what we as a city, state, and nation accomplished by rebuilding and rising from the ashes of that horrific day.

CHAPTER 11

GOVERNMENT IS NOT THE SOLUTION TO OUR PROBLEM; GOVERNMENT IS THE PROBLEM

Confucius wrote, "Our greatest glory is not in never falling, but in rising every time we fall."

In life, most of us do whatever it takes to get back up and get going again. Some people need a life coach. Others need a change of pace. Some require a radical departure from their lifestyle.

But what comes after? What do you do once you've been knocked down and gotten back up? You learn. You learn from your mistakes and correct the path you were on.

Politically, the first thing we need to do is acknowledge that both Republicans and Democrats, and certainly a polarized and political "news media," helped foster the toxic environment we now live in. We are divided, and we are angry. Americans may never embrace post-9/11-style patriotism and gushing love for one another again, but we can and must return to basic civility.

In the past few years, from the man who attempted to assassinate House Republicans on a baseball field to a deranged individual who mailed pipe bombs to prominent Democrats, people have become engaged in an entirely new fanatical realm of political factions. It's clear that fanatics on both the left and the right are willing to engage in violence over politics. These people are no better than the hijackers of 9/11.

There are ways we can return to a more civil society. Some of those include political solutions; others demand more self-awareness on the left and right. Allow me to start with the really big picture.

Restoring Trust in Government

THERE ARE TWO THINGS THAT MUST BE DONE IF WE ARE TO HEAL our fractured country. First, we have to restore the people's belief that Washington is their government, regardless of which party is in control. Second, the people must trust that our government will face up to and solve the challenges our country faces today.

Government Is Too Big

THE GOVERNMENT GETS INVOLVED IN WAY TOO MUCH. WHEN IT does, even under the direction of people with good intentions, its solutions become problematic, often ending up detrimental to society. Please, if you consider yourself a Democrat, a liberal, or a moderate Republican, don't shoot those words down as talking points. Hear me out.

When the federal government is involved in almost every aspect of our life, it's no wonder we get irrationally furious about what those in Washington do—what they leave in or out, what stays or what gets cut.

Something uniquely American is that we have a simultaneous working relationship *with* and a healthy distrust *of* our federal government. It has worked well for more than two hundred years. But these days, it's disheartening to watch the left demand more government involvement in our daily lives. It's mind-blowing that these same people calling for heavy-handed government intervention in health care, housing, and education are the same ones screaming that Donald Trump is a fascist on the path to a dictatorship. Those on the right are equally guilty. They call for checks and balances, and when President Trump issues executive orders, it's fine. But when Obama carried out his agenda, the right jeered and the left cheered. This is a fundamental disconnect I will never understand. The same people demanding more government are the ones *living in fear of it.*

I get as upset as anyone else when it comes to unilateral executive orders, such as a president's changing a law or applying different types of policy. That's exactly why I prefer more local control, taking power out of the hands of a select few in Washington. Government is too big and too involved. It needs to release its grip on our economy and get out of our personal lives. This would stop us from fighting over whose "side" gets to control all of that power.

After all, when the government isn't picking sides, there's no side to be on. There are no winners or losers.

Lobbying

WITH WASHINGTON IN CONTROL OVER SO MUCH IN OUR DAILY lives, aside from lawmakers, there's another large group of people who will do everything they can to influence, shape, and affect decisions that directly impact us and our children's lives: lobbyists. Let's be clear: the lobbyists aren't doing anything wrong, certainly nothing illegal. They're paid to influence government. But the consequences of their actions are wrong. The rich and powerful do undoubtedly influence most government decisions. The government too often acts in their interest and not the people's.

While it is abundantly clear that government is too big, I also believe government can and should have strict oversight in some areas, including lobbying. Let's look at why lobbyists exist.

Quite simply, lobbyists exist to influence government decisions affecting the lives of all of us. The people who are employed by our ever-expanding government are involved in our daily lives and in entire industries every time they set the framework for who gets tax breaks, tax incentives, or under Democrats, tax increases. They decide who gets regulated and who doesn't. In effect, the federal government creates jobs for lobbyists.

If an industry or a business is looking for funding from the government, whether it's for research and development by way of a grant or indirect money through tax incentives, a lobbyist has to persuade members of Congress, White House staff, or the president directly. With government being so massive, the stakes have become astronomically high. A simple line put in or left out of a thousand-page bill can mean hundreds of millions of dollars to an industry. If government were not involved in picking winners and losers in these industries, there would be no reason to lobby.

When we learn about these perks and handouts, we get furious. Immediately, like everything else, we break it down to "my side or yours," Republican or Democrat. But if you want the government to quit picking sides, stop the handouts. Stop the enormous extent of special tax treatment that exists today.

I get that it's not that simple, at least for those of us not purely libertarian. As a governor, I understand that choices need to be made, and sometimes those choices are made along philosophical boundaries relating to one side of the aisle or the other. My larger point is that when the government is overreaching and involved in too many aspects of our lives, with literally trillions of dollars on the line, lobbyists have far too many reasons to be involved.

So, with that said, here are a few bipartisan solutions that do not tilt Washington left or right, while getting a handle on out-of-control lobbying in Washington.

A key to stopping corruption in Washington is to ban interest groups that benefit from lobbying from participating in political campaigns. This is as bipartisan as you can get. Republicans would love to ban unions and trial lawyers from lobbying. Democrats want the US Chamber of Commerce and oil companies out of politics. But to pass this kind of legislation, you need to do both.

It's no wonder that Americans have grown so suspect about their government. It is not theirs. No private or public company that lobbies should be allowed to contribute to a campaign or engage in any political activity, and neither should that company's employees.

At face value, this should be obvious. "Hello, Mr. Smith. Welcome to Washington. You're welcome for the tens of thousands of dollars we pumped into getting you elected! Now, we'd like to talk about legislation you're going to pass for us."

Powerful interests in Washington, from unions to private companies to entire industries, have a disproportionate influence on the country's lawmaking process. Whatever organization, company, union, or trade association that benefits directly or indirectly from the services of a lobbyist should be precluded from being involved in campaigns. The current situation is inherently corrupt, and it happens on both sides of the aisle. Teachers' unions, which have a stranglehold on the Democrats, trap minority kids in hideously bad schools. Big oil companies pin down Republicans and make sure they vote to keep our precious water and sensitive environmental areas open for drilling. This must stop.

Federal employees have to follow what's called the Hatch Act, which is a law preventing them from overtly participating in political events and activities. Similar laws that apply to anyone engaging in lobbying could be enacted. Free speech under our constitution entitles groups to lobby our government or to participate in political campaigns. But no provision permits them to do both. Want to hire a lobbyist? Fine, but you can't donate or spend on campaigns. Do you want to spend endless amounts on campaigns? No problem, but you cannot hire a lobbyist to influence those you just helped get elected. It is constitutional, and it helps make the government *our government again.*

Ultimately, the solution is to have a smaller, less powerful government in which the stakes aren't so high that the rich and powerful can buy influence. To see how wealthy, powerful, and abundant lobbying has become, look at the suburbs of Washington. The top three wealthiest counties in the nation today surround DC. That is not a coincidence. The cost of rent in DC has skyrocketed; housing prices are through the roof. An abundance of wealth is circulating around the nation's capital at the expense of you, the taxpayer—directly with your money and by wealthy corporations, unions, and other organizations trying to influence where *your money* goes.

Ban Members of Congress from Lobbying

A SECOND STEP TO CONTROL LOBBYING AND RETURN TRUST IN government would be to ban members of Congress from lobbying for life. Hundreds of former members of the House and Senate are registered lobbyists. Do you know that there are more former members of Congress registered as lobbyists in Washington today than are currently serving in Congress? That's not right! If you serve in the House or Senate, you should be banned for the rest of your life from working as a lobbyist. This would go a long way toward ending the perpetual inside nature of Washington politics, where the connected represent the connected.

When members are done serving in Washington, they should go back home to the people who sent them there. But many don't. Many work diligently while serving to become as connected as they can to specific industries and to the lobbyists that serve those interests. They do this knowing they are never, ever going to leave Washington, where high-paying jobs will be lined up for them right after their time in Congress. This directly affects what they do daily, including how they vote and how they wield their influence. Most important, it impacts the people's sense of fairness in our government.

End the inside game. Restore people's faith in government.

CHAPTER 11

Limitless Dollars, Total Transparency

THE ARGUMENT FOR CAMPAIGN-FINANCE REFORM IS USELESS, petty, and irrelevant. Does that sound crazy? Read on.

In 2016, outside groups spent $1 billion—yes, $1,000,000,000—trying to influence the elections that year. Some groups can take unlimited contributions, not only from individuals but from corporations as well. But candidates were limited to only $2,700 at a time from individual donors. During the next cycle, it got bumped up a full one hundred bucks, to $2,800.

Republicans and Democrats scream all day about limiting lobbyists' money in politics while taking money from lobbyists. Then, in a purely symbolic move, politicians come up with these arbitrary limits on donations to campaigns. As I said, the current maximum donation you can give to a federal candidate's campaign is $2,800. But what if you donate $2,801? That is illegal, and apparently, that extra dollar is the key to unlocking everything you want from the government. That one dollar allows you to cross the threshold into holding your member of Congress hostage and demanding whatever you want.

It's arbitrary, and it doesn't work. So, what do we do, just allow unlimited amounts of money to be injected into politics? The fact is, we already do!

That single dollar over $2,800 somehow signifies corruption and undue influence, yet a corporation, a union, or even one wealthy individual can donate *twenty-eight million dollars* to a political action committee, better known as a PAC. It makes no sense. In this way, these powerful interests spend hundreds of millions of dollars to influence the outcome of an election without donating a nickel to a candidate directly.

The rules, regulations, and arbitrary limits are a charade. Hypocritically, some of the loudest "progressive" voices proudly proclaiming their purity from PAC donations have no problem when it comes to Tom Steyer, George Soros, or other outside groups spending hundreds of millions to support them and their causes.

These rules are set up to be poked, prodded, moved around, and altered by high-priced election lawyers. The politicians know this. Still, they continue to talk about the unholy influence of money in politics while their hand is out asking for more.

Contributions should not have any arbitrary limits on them. However, they must be made entirely transparent, and as quickly as possible. Candidates should be required to disclose where the money comes from and make all contributions above one hundred dollars visible on a website, both their own and that of the Federal Election Commission, within a twenty-four-hour time frame.

Media

Exacerbating our cultural divisions, there's another group thoroughly loved by the American public almost as much as lobbyists—the media.

The media—traditional and social—are tearing us apart. And frankly, we are to blame. We buy what they're selling. We click, like, share, and advance lies and nonsensical conspiracy theories that pass as news.

President Trump, at political rallies and on Twitter, has called media "the enemy of the people." He claims he uses that phrase only when addressing the "fake news" media. If you ask Democrats, he is exactly like the late Venezuelan dictator Hugo Chávez, who revoked licenses and shut down all private media organizations that were critical of him. If you ask Trump supporters how they feel about the press, they'll say they want notoriously confrontational CNN reporter Jim Acosta sent to Gitmo for infinite sessions of waterboarding.

The press is not the enemy of the people. A free press is a critical component of our democracy, enshrined in our First Amendment. Simultaneously, comparing Trump to Chávez is a grave offense to victims in Venezuela, a country that has fallen into complete chaos, with infant mortality rates rivaling those of the war-torn country of Syria.

It's hard to take journalists seriously when they decry Trump as the next Chávez yet treated President Obama with kid gloves. Obama targeted journalists for retribution with the tacit support of Attorney General Eric Holder and still got a pass from the media. The Obama administration slapped reporters with subpoenas in an attempt to get them to reveal their sources, spied on reporters, and labeled a Fox News journalist an "unindicted coconspirator" for doing nothing more than reporting the news.

Even Obama's hometown paper, the *Chicago Tribune*, acknowledged this reality when it wrote: "Shocked by Trump aggression against reporters and sources? The blueprint was made by Obama." The article was relegated to the commentary section, though. In other words, it was an op-ed, not a news item listing the aforementioned facts.

As much as I harp on Washington's politicians, journalists need to take a long look in the mirror.

According to a study by Indiana University professors, only 7 percent of journalists identify as Republican. The rest identify as either Democrat or Independent. While there are some fine journalists who do report all sides to a story, the news is so overwhelmingly left leaning, it's not a stretch to think that those Independents are about as independent as Bernie Sanders, the Independent senator of Vermont, who caucuses with Democrats and runs for president as a Democratic Socialist. Although to be fair to Bernie, he doesn't identify as a Democrat because they're not far enough left for him.

The media's coverage of Donald Trump has been overwhelmingly negative. I thoroughly understand that the president brings this on himself needlessly and foolishly. But you cannot deny that, at a minimum, Republican economic policy—tax reform and regulatory relief—has been a clear success. The president talks up the fact that the economy is booming, with record low unemployment levels, but he is often dismissed or ignored. If a Democrat were in office with these numbers, most especially the record low minority unemployment levels across the country, that president would be hailed a hero whose policies benefited the working class. Yet we rarely hear about the economy. Instead, we get "breaking news" on what Donald Trump tweeted moments ago, followed by hours of panel discussions with pundits assessing, analyzing, and criticizing each and every character of that tweet.

In a report about the media's coverage of Trump in his first few months in office, the nonpartisan Pew Research Center released statistics showing it was overwhelmingly negative. Broken down by time and content, the study found coverage to be three times more negative than that of President Obama. It was twice as negative compared to that of former presidents Bush and Clinton.

Journalists, like everyone else, are entitled to their opinions. But some in the media today don't even know they lean one way or another. Many live in bubbles, specifically in Washington and New York. They are surrounded by people at work, cocktail parties, coffee shops—everywhere, really—who reinforce their beliefs on a daily basis.

We cannot have a democracy with journalists whose only purpose is to reinforce their preexisting, narrow, and partisan mindset. This applies to the left and the right. While most of the media is overwhelmingly liberal, allow me to be an equal-opportunity shot taker and call out both sides of the spectrum, not just MSNBC and HuffPost but Fox News and Breitbart as well. Oftentimes the newscasts and their prime-time political pundits are there simply to serve as comforting voices in echo chambers, giving no context, history, or nuance. Instead, we get ideology masquerading as news.

Our news media is failing the American people because of its partisanship and ideology. Worse, this translates directly into advocacy, and when you have advocates instead of journalists, you have people on one side who will feel targeted by the media. The targets feel victimized. Soon after, the trust fades.

Nowadays, news outlets advance a partisan or ideological agenda based simply on what they choose to cover in the first place. Consider the examples of Fox and MSNBC—when a specific type of news event happens, it's often newsworthy to one station but irrelevant to the other.

It's not just *how* they present the news; it's *whether* they present the news at all. Today the American people don't trust the media, but it is still the source for their information. Our democracy is threatened when there is no objective source of news that the people can trust.

Free Speech and Civil Discourse

DEMOCRACY REQUIRES TOLERATING AND ENCOURAGING A DIVERSITY of opinions, including ones you find completely unacceptable. Today's left is working overtime to delegitimize certain ideas, philosophies, and speech, and the media is silent about it. Let's look at some of the places and ways in which this is taking place.

Academia

UNIVERSITIES USED TO BE BASTIONS OF FREE THOUGHT AND debate, run by classic liberals. But now, professors and administrators, pressured by social-justice warriors, are shutting down speakers, debate, and at the most basic level, the exchange of ideas. The free flow of discussion and ideas is considered to be politically polarizing or hurtful for some campus groups. Overwhelmingly, conservative speakers are targeted for protests, or their events get canceled before the speakers have even arrived on campus. Certain speakers are considered illegitimate or dangerous because of their often mundane, noncontroversial, traditional political ideology.

I wish those in the press, whose entire existence hangs on free speech, would take a hard look at how they are ignoring what is happening on campuses throughout the United States. Intolerant leftists, who hold some of the highest, most powerful positions at universities, are shutting down free speech and degrading the true meaning of diversity.

Conservatives from Ann Coulter to Ben Shapiro have been at the epicenter of violent protests on some campuses. Leftists have also shouted down and tried to silence even seemingly innocuous speakers, some who have chosen not to label themselves along party lines.

Take, for example, Dave Rubin. He hosts a popular online talk show, *The Rubin Report*. On paper, you'd take one look and say this guy has to be a liberal Democrat. Born in Brooklyn, New York, Dave grew up with his Jewish family on Long Island. He moved to Manhattan, where he started his career as a stand-up comic. He made his way into media, interning at *The Daily Show with Jon Stewart*. Later, he worked for the progressive, far-left online show *The Young Turks*.

This freakin' guy's gotta be a freedom-hating lib, right?

Quite the contrary.

Dave is an independent-minded critical thinker who has become one of the country's most prominent fighters for free speech, inclusion, and open-minded dialogue. And that, ironically, is his problem.

Dave moved to Los Angeles to start his namesake program. On his show, he took on "controversial" themes, like supporting the First Amendment and advocating for a smaller, less intrusive government. Pretty radical, huh? Dave committed a sin when he allowed people on his show who he didn't always agree with; neither did the left. He dared to offer something unique—dialogue. *Oh no!* Dave also had the guts to host guests who disagreed with each other. They debated, exchanging ideas and thoughts in a civil manner. *Criminal!* Soon after, the left blacklisted him. *Yes! Castigate that evil man!*

Dave committed the unholy sin of "giving platforms" to people the left disagreed with, and that led to pundits and social media mobs going after him with a vengeance. The openly gay man was deemed antigay. The tolerant, open-minded, and accepting Dave

Rubin—the kind of guy everyone gets along with—was labeled a hateful far-right extremist.

After challenging media norms and our country's tribal expectations, Dave's show grew in popularity; so did demand for him. He began speaking at universities all over the country. At a college in New Hampshire, he learned quickly about civility from the left as he tried to have a civil conversation, touching on the aforementioned themes.

In May 2018, Dave spoke to a group of about three hundred students at the University of New Hampshire. The group was diverse, made up of conservatives, liberals, and others with no philosophical or political association. Many were there simply to hear him speak and engage in interesting conversation. Dave started, and in the first few minutes, so did the protestors.

"Black lives matter! Black lives matter! Black lives matter! Black lives matter! Black lives matter! Black lives matter! Black lives matter! Black lives matter!"

I don't have the ink, pages, or time in this book to keep copying and pasting that phrase. But the protestors had all night. The two white protesting students droned on.

"Black lives matter! Black lives matter! Black lives matter!"

Dave stopped his speech and went out of his way to engage them. He offered them the microphone to air their grievances. He literally tried to pass the mic.

"Black lives matter! Black lives matter! Black lives matter!"

He asked, "Do you think I don't think black lives matter?"

No answer. Only, "Black lives matter!"

Dave begged them to say anything at all except…

"Black lives matter! Black lives matter! Black lives matter!"

But they continued.

Eventually, they were stopped. Dave's speech went on.

He continued talking about his highly racist, extremist agenda of inclusion and acceptance. And then…

Clink. Clink. Clink.

"Umm," the interrupted Dave said, looking into the crowd to see where the noise was coming from. Another protestor was at it, sitting in the crowd with a blank stare, shaking a jar full of quarters, dimes, nickels, and pennies.

"Is this a local thing?" a confused Dave asked.

Clink. Clink. Clink.

Once again, Dave tried. He tried hard to get the woman, with a blank stare and no emotion, to speak. No such luck.

Clink. Clink. Clink.

No matter how trivial, random, or plain stupid these protestors' tactics were, they had one serious goal in mind—to shut Dave up. They wanted to stifle his right to speak and share his personal opinions.

Dave rolled on. Not for long, though.

Another shout came from the crowd: "We don't want you in the LGBT community! Get the fuck out!"

Whoa! This was anger!

Dave, an openly gay man, was told to get the eff out because the LGBT community didn't want him. Dave was barely into his speech—again touching on radical themes like *inclusion and diversity*—and here he was facing the third protestor trying to shut him down.

Now, as if stifling free speech, especially speech about inclusion and freedom, weren't shocking enough, the person who launched this tirade should absolutely shock you. The obviously angry woman in the back continued screaming, accusing Rubin of being hostile to transgender rights. Rubin responded with more of his crazy-ass, radical agenda about inclusion and diversity.

"I am one hundred percent for you to have the same exact dignity as everyone else in this country. And I am one hundred percent for you to have every law and legal protection that anyone else in this country has. So, what is it that you don't want me to say that I have said here?"

No answer from the protestor. Instead Dave got, "Why are you seeking to support misgendering people?"

He answered with some far-out stuff: "In free Western societies, you have the right to free speech. You don't have the right to not be offended."

Then Dave addressed what the protestor was really asking for—creating laws: "Think about what you're calling for here. What you're saying is that if someone walking down the street misgenders, you want this person to be fined or put in jail. That's what you think is right?"

No answer.

Dave ended the confrontation and tried to make amends with a passionate, heartfelt speech.

> If the government started cracking down on you because you happen to be trans, I will be your biggest ally! I will be out there with you every day. So, you really need to be careful what you ask for. I get it. You're coming from a place where you don't want to be hurt. Nobody wants to be hurt, right? Everybody has had bad shit said about them. Everyone's got something they're insecure about. Everyone's got it. But believe me, the idea that the government is going to solve that problem—it is not the way to go.

Rubin wrapped up by looking for common ground, asking, "Did we get anywhere?"

The shouter shook her head no and left the room. But then, she got him good. Oh, she got him really good. Like a child, the middle-aged woman logged on to Twitter and tweet-stormed: "We did something right! Glad we were able to disrupt this man's hate speech as much as possible. He is nothing but a provocateur and 'civil discourse' with him is impossible."

The loud, petulant, childlike protester who tweeted that was Doctor Joelle Ruby Ryan, a professor at the University of New Hampshire. A professor! She identifies as trans and is listed as a senior lecturer in women's studies at the university. Her courses include Introduction to Women's Studies; Gender, Power, and Privilege; and Transgender Feminism. Her specialties, again according to the school, are as follows: transgender/LGBTQ, film/media, sex work, disability justice, fat studies, and social movements.

This is a professor who educates, or maybe more appropriately said, indoctrinates young men and women every day. Aside from my obvious trepidations and fears that this professor encourages marginalizing and flat-out shutting down anyone who remotely goes against her beliefs, there's something more we should be worried about. The University of New Hampshire *allowed* this kind of fascist behavior from students and a professor.

There are no consequences, not for the violent Antifa protestors on other college campuses or this professor trying to shut down Dave. Nothing matters, because college disciplinarians and administrators aren't doing a thing. Worse, they're encouraging it!

We all need to encourage and celebrate free speech. It is a cornerstone of American society. It's what makes us unique and one of the strongest nations on earth. Unbelievably, the media ignores what's happening. We are watching an entire generation that preaches diversity shut it down the moment they're uncomfortable with it. Diversity is great, unless it comes to diversity of political thought! Some ideas simply can't be expressed. This is terrifying.

I ask journalists working now: What will you do when these children become lawmakers or hold other powerful positions? They won't take too kindly to your stories and reporting, because they don't have the emotional or rational capability to handle anyone challenging their belief system. And challenging the powerful is what your entire existence is built on.

Antifa

IN OUR COMPLETELY TWISTED WORLD, THE REAL BAD GUYS PERPETRATING violence and throwing firebombs at businesses and police officers are somehow hailed as principled protestors. CNN talking head Don Lemon became a parody of himself one night by suggesting, "It says it right in the name: Antifa. Antifascism." You have to have a serious disregard of facts to say something that utterly insane. He added, "Listen, no organization is perfect."

Equally as insane is that this black-clad, mask-wearing group calls itself Antifa, again, short for "Antifascists." These brave antifascists shut down speakers, stifle the exchange of ideas, and violently disrupt people who hold different opinions. In other words, the antifascists engage in fascist acts. *They are the very definition of "fascist."*

And it's not just faceless Antifa members. It's people openly committing acts of aggression against anyone with a conservative bent or, God forbid, a certain shirt or hat. In fact, wearing one particular dreaded and feared piece of paraphernalia is the equivalent of wrapping yourself in a Nazi flag and running around with a burning cross—the MAGA hat! *Gasp! Oh my God!* Yes. Bad. I know. A tacky-looking hat with the phrase "Make America Great Again" is now synonymous with white supremacy. Go to a college campus with an Obama T-shirt, a Hillary sign, or an Elizabeth Warren bumper sticker on your car and you will have no issue at all. Hell, sport a T-shirt with an image of Che Guevara (a man who was racist, homophobic, and a mass murderer) and you'll get high fives. But try wearing a MAGA hat on that same campus and see what the consequences are. You might get your head kicked in.

Hate Speech

ON COLLEGE CAMPUSES AND IN CERTAIN CIRCLES ON THE LEFT, some are calling for hate speech laws. What is hate speech? It's obvious. Hate speech is simply someone else's opinion. It might be a statement that contradicts another person's beliefs. In other words, it's free speech.

Those on the left need to wake up and realize that laws created to shut people down they do *not* agree with *today* can and will be used to shut down people they *do* agree with *tomorrow*.

Look at it retrospectively. Hate speech laws could have easily been applied to someone like the great Martin Luther King. Powerful elected officials, from local sheriffs to governors, most especially in the South, could have easily abused these types of "hate speech" laws to arrest, shut down, and permanently silence someone like MLK, who was considered a radical in his time for speaking out about civil rights.

Now, groups associated with the left, like Black Lives Matter, are even attacking other left-leaning groups. In one recent example of the left's eating the left, an American Civil Liberties Union (ACLU) speaker was aggressively shouted at and shut down on a college campus. Take a look at the title and subtitle of an article in *Reason* magazine and see if your head explodes:

> *Black Lives Matter Students Shut Down the ACLU's Campus Free Speech Event Because 'Liberalism Is White Supremacy'*

> *"The revolution will not uphold the Constitution."*

In the article, reporter Robby Soave writes about how students in the group Black Lives Matter barged in on an event at the College of William & Mary to shut down the ACLU. The ACLU speaker was presenting on "Students and the First Amendment." Once again, pretty radical stuff, huh?

Soave writes, "Protesters drowned her out with cries of, 'ACLU, you protect Hitler, too.'" They also chanted, "The oppressed are not impressed," and finished with another impressively stupid statement: "Liberalism is white supremacy."

Nadine Strossen, author and former ACLU president, summed up the ignorance and arrogance perfectly in an interview focusing on her book *Hate: Why We Should Resist It with Free Speech, Not Censorship.* Strossen laid out why the left in particular should shun attempts to shut down free speech: "Every crusader for racial justice throughout our history has also been a very strong free speech champion—Frederick Douglass, W. E. B. Du Bois, Martin Luther King—and one of the reasons was that in their time, in the places where they were advocating, their speech was attacked as hateful and dangerous and threatening social stability and the very ongoing survival of the nation itself."

On some large and prominent college campuses, conservative speakers are being physically threatened and physically accosted, or having their events canceled, because the intolerant left says their views are illegitimate.

Imagine if a left-wing professor were to go to speak at a campus, and a bunch of conservative right-wing males shut him or her down or physically threatened that person. How much attention do you think that would get? It would be on every front page. And what would the consequences be? This has happened constantly to conservative speakers on campuses, yet it gets little national attention. When certain thoughts are considered illegitimate, it is a grave threat to our democracy.

A New Lexicon

NEWLY INVENTED WORDS HAVE ALSO MADE THEIR WAY INTO THE American lexicon to further delegitimize people. Two examples you hear often these days are "mansplaining" and "white privilege." Here's what those phrases mean: Based on your gender and race, what you're saying is irrelevant; you are disqualified from having an opinion on a matter.

Oftentimes the people who use these terms don't refute the logic of what someone is saying. Rather, they disqualify it because of the person who's making the statement. Wouldn't it be a little better to engage and try to intellectually discuss the value of the thought as opposed to disqualifying the speaker?

Information Overload

YOU CANNOT HAVE A DEMOCRACY WHEN A POLITICIZED, IDEOLOGICAL media doesn't consider all the things I've just discussed important. But then again, in the new media landscape, the only thing that's important is what is happening right here, right now, in the moment. How can anyone keep up?

In our constantly connected world, I try to imagine the amount of information any given journalist receives in one day.

Wake up. Read the paper online or the old-fashioned way. Flip on the morning news. Check email. Check Twitter. Check direct messages on Twitter. Check texts. Check Instagram for a fun thirty-second break and just in case someone sent a message in that app. Check Facebook to see what the Russians are circulating that day and what crazy stories a conservative grandfather or liberal hippie uncle has shared. Again, check it to make sure no one has messaged there either. Any missed calls? Missed texts? If not, by seven in the morning, they're bound to roll in soon.

Taking in, absorbing, and disseminating information *with context* must be as challenging for a reporter as it is for the public.

Now, more than ever, we are inundated with video, images, and words coming at us by the second. Everything is recorded, uploaded, and blasted out for the world to see via TV, computer, mobile device, and app. Every second of every day, we sort through thousands of images, words, reports, and videos with our faces stuck in mobile devices.

The news is no longer informed dialogue with perspective or context. *It's gluttony!* It's one of the seven deadly sins. The media is providing it on traditional and digital platforms, the public is helping dish it out on social media, and we're all stuffing our faces with it like a buffet.

In our hyperfast, hyperconnected world, there's no making sense of it. Just take it all in and live through the outrage of the moment. We're voyeurs, reveling in the pain and hurt of others.

Being on social media is like taking a hit of a drug or pulling the lever on a slot machine. Every hour, minute, and second, with every click, punch, and swipe to refresh browsers, pages, apps, and mobile devices, we get a massive hit of dopamine to the brain.

On social media, we're not only voyeurs passively watching TV; we're psychiatrists to those we love and bullies to those we hate. We get active, taking shots at people we don't like. Only a decade ago, no one could have imagined that you would see an iconic news anchor like Dan Rather or actor like Mark Hamill spouting off on Twitter. Nor could anyone imagine the trolling, defiling, and mocking that you could dish right back at that celebrity.

Informed dialogue doesn't exist in social media. It's a place for the tribes to disseminate propaganda, discredit the other side's information, and do so while crapping all over one another.

Democracy requires an informed electorate that has the chance to see and hear all sides to a story. But information with context and perspective is nearly impossible to come by when the media reports only on the most recent political car crash, which is typically a nasty over-the-top tweet sent by Trump that morning or a bombastic statement made by Representative Maxine Waters an hour later. There's no filter. It's a race to cover any given outrage as fast as possible. And soon after, the news networks arrange a table-top of pundits to pop off on how great, terrible, kind, or awful a person or subject is.

Solutions

REPUBLICANS AND DEMOCRATS HAVE TO COME TOGETHER TO advance solutions, but the only way they will do that is if they recognize basic facts. Right now, statistics and science are being denied by both parties or worse, twisted to make political gains.

The climate is getting warmer. Public education in some parts of America is an abject failure. Immigration policy, for those who try to come here legally and those residing here illegally, is a mess. And too many Americans are simply too dependent on government. These are real problems that will never get solved unless both parties work together.

Our elected officials must work together to advance solutions that are practical, while expanding economic opportunity.

The Climate

Even in our hyperpartisan environment, you would think some issues are above the political fray. Now, I understand that voters who care only about one issue have always existed. Abortion and guns are two prominent examples of these issues. Depending on which side they sit on, some people will vote for or against candidates based on their stances on these hot-button topics. In our hyperpartisan world, though, people are putting more and more issues in the same fanatical realm as abortion and guns. A prominent example is the environment.

There was a time when the discussion on climate change was an intelligent conversation about appropriate responses based on possible risks. Now climate change is a religion, and if you dare break its tenets, you are a heretic who should be burned at the stake. The conversation has gone from looking for rational conclusions to pledging loyalty to a religious doctrine. Once you stop thinking rationally about a problem and possible solutions and turn the issue into a cult with blind ideology, the solution often becomes worse than the problem.

Government can and should play a sensible role as a steward of the environment, and that includes dealing with climate change. Both major parties and all political ideologies must recognize that a healthy environment means a healthy economy, and both can thrive together. I went into government hoping to leave a better state behind for future generations, and leaving an enhanced natural environment is a critical part of that.

As New York's governor, I led the creation of the Regional Greenhouse Gas Initiative. It required large emitters of carbon dioxide (CO_2), primarily utilities, to gradually lower their emissions. It was the first cap-and-trade program for CO2 emissions in the country. The idea was to take intelligent steps, consistent with economic growth, to reduce emissions. The best part is that it was driven by the states, not Washington. The multistate program included almost all of New England, New York, Delaware, and New Jersey. The only state that wouldn't join us at the time was Massachusetts. Governor Mitt Romney, while at first a strong supporter, had his sights set on something apparently more important to him. Romney was going to run for president.

The agreement was bipartisan, showing that Democrats and Republicans could work together to enact policies that didn't decimate business or burden people with overwhelming taxes or regulations, all while doing the right thing for the environment. Unfortunately, the split on environmental issues is another symptom of our illness in America. As the left has become more aggressive with environmental policy and the rhetoric revolving around it, the right has pushed back hard, attempting to wipe away as many regulations as possible. Both sides remain willfully blind and ignorant. Democrats have no regard for the real-world cost of implementing heavy-handed regulations. Republicans seem to bend over backward to support drilling and fossil fuels, not even entertaining the idea that some research and development of technologies to mitigate climate change could pay off in large economic dividends.

An American solution isn't going to prevent CO_2 emissions from warming the planet. A global solution that includes China, India, and other large emitters is essential, but America can and should lead. Today, the US emits less than 17 percent of the world's CO_2. Of the more than 5,000 coal-fired plants in the world, fewer than 250 are in the US. We could shut down every one and within a decade there would still be more coal plants than there are today.

The natural gas boom, created by fracking, has allowed coal and oil power plants to be replaced with cleaner natural gas, dramatically reducing emissions. It's why we lead the world in CO_2 reductions.

We should also incentivize solutions such as advanced storage technologies. This would allow intermittent clean wind and solar power to be stored and used consistently, not just when the sun shines or the wind blows. Promising solutions, driven by social concern, could be achieved by encouraging and funding reforestation of the Sub-Saharan Sahel. Reforestation would absorb CO2, green the landscape, and create opportunities for an economically impoverished part of the world.

Studies show that reforestation, meaning greening the planet by planting billions of trees, would reverse the high level of CO2 in the atmosphere today. Technologies that pull CO2 from the atmosphere with nanocoated metallic surfaces can clean the air and create new resources. Transportation breakthroughs, whether using hydrogen, fuel cell, biofuels, or electric sources, could further reduce emissions, grow our economy, and be exported globally.

The list is endless but the point is clear: intelligent ideas can advance a global solution to protect the planet and expand economic opportunity. The US should incentivize technological innovation, and in the process, reduce emissions while exporting new technologies. America will create jobs at home while advancing a global solution to global warming.

So, let's take a deep breath. The world is not going to end anytime soon, and yes, cows that fart and planes that fly still have a place on the planet. However, changing the atmosphere by adding large amounts of CO2 will ultimately affect our climate. Solutions are there. The dialogue is not.

When you have subjects that become relegated to one side or the other—Democrat or Republican—eventually the proposed solutions become worse than the problem. Or the sides simply stop offering any solutions at all.

Our elected officials, regardless of party, must address what is clearly an issue and then show a skeptical public that our government can work together for the future of the planet.

Education and Inequality

LET'S TALK ABOUT INEQUALITY. IT'S A WORD THE LEFT USES OFTEN without a clear definition of what it means or reasonable solutions to address it. For years, Democrats have deployed class warfare campaigns, creating resentment over success instead of celebrating it. In turn, their solutions focus more on penalizing the wealthy instead of helping the poor. It's about bringing the rich down and not raising lower-income people up. The word inequality now functions as a political tool for the left, even as the economy soars. Allow me to explain one of the major reasons why we have inequality in this country, on display every day in America—our failing education system.

For the vast majority of students, our public education system is a blessing. In the morning, parents drop their kids off at school or leave them at the bus stop, and at the end of the day, they come home. The kids have learned something new, they're happy, and they're on their way to a brighter future. But for families in low-income neighborhoods—and minorities in particular—it's a radically different story.

We trap minority kids in horrible schools and don't give them the slightest chance to escape. We don't even entertain providing them with a most basic privilege—a choice. This is America. We have choices for everything, *unless you're a poor minority kid trapped in an awful school.*

What's worse is that the only solution ever put forth by Democrats year after year is to throw more money at the problem. Hint: that has never worked. They go after successful people and shake them down for more of their hard-earned dollars. They demand higher taxes, saying more of it will "go to the kids." They do this at the same time that they have unequivocally denied opportunity to millions of low-income students—particularly inner-city African Americans—by insisting on failing public schools and failing teachers. This is immoral. It is a travesty.

Imagine white Republican politicians saying, "We're not going to let black kids go to this public school. We're going to require them to go to one that is far worse." It sure sounds a lot like the 1950s South. Incredibly, it's exactly what's happening, but the Democrats are doing it, so it's somehow acceptable. These Democrats are beholden and captive to teachers' unions, which funnel money into their campaigns to get them elected. Just as sickening, the media rarely questions any of it.

We should have public schools that give all children a chance to achieve their dreams to the extent of their ability and their willingness to work. We should not have teachers who can't teach, and we should stop rewarding schools that are abject failures. We should give the parents of those kids an alternative. Yet somehow, for some reason, this is controversial. *Why? How?*

What is undoubtedly controversial is that for fifty years we have been sending low-income black kids to schools that fail. Their teachers can't teach, either because they are inept or because the environment is so terrible that it's impossible to do so. And those who won't teach or don't have the capacity to do so are never held responsible. Democrats, who claim they work to protect these students, are so beholden to the teachers' unions that they won't allow the worst of the worst to be reprimanded, and firing them is out of the question. This is an international disgrace. Elected leaders need to demand change. But they don't. They won't.

During President Obama's first term, while his daughters attended the best private school in DC, he had the audacity to shut down a voucher program for students in Washington. The program had given vouchers to low-income DC students, allowing them to leave their low-performing public school and attend a successful private school. The White House put out a statement saying, "The Federal Government should focus its attention and available resources on improving the quality of public schools for all students." Good luck with that. Spending increases every single year (that is, more "resources" are allocated) to try to improve those schools, with little success.

Let me offer three solutions to help students and improve schools.

First, make sure that teachers actually know the subject they are supposed to teach. In New York, this was and is a major problem. Our schools should require periodic testing of teachers in the subject area in which they are educating students. If they fail, don't fire them. Instead, give them a semester-long training program and then test again. If they cannot pass, then they should be removed.

Second, create an education tax credit for parents under a certain income level who have kids in failing schools. If the school is deemed to be subpar, if it resides in a low-income district, and if the parents' income is below a specific threshold, the parents should get a tax credit for after-school tutor programs in any subject they choose. Furthermore, these credits should be able to be used toward private or public schools.

The concept behind this policy does something that too few policies reinforce. It empowers people.

You empower parents to pick and choose, and more important, get involved in their children's lives. Every study, whether it's conducted by a left- or right-leaning organization, indicates that a child's educational success is directly related to parental involvement. This idea involves the parent because the mom or dad makes the decision on how to best use that tax-credit money to enhance his or her child's education. It empowers the children because if they are really good at something and want to do more of it, they can put the credit toward tutoring or summer programs. It creates an alternative to a failing public school.

The credits could also be applied to college preparation. Think about the students who attend SAT or ACT prep classes. They're often kids from wealthy families. The parents have the disposable income to send their child to these classes to gear up for the college entrance exams. These are the kids who already have access to either a high-performing public school in a wealthy part of town or an ultra-rich private school. The poor kids don't have this kind of access. A tax-credit policy might not result in equal footing, but it certainly would give them more of a chance.

The third solution is to greatly expand charter school programs. I enacted the charter law in New York but now Democrats, beholden to unions, want to limit and close charter schools. Why? They work! Students are doing well, but Democrats will not allow the monopoly status to be challenged. This mistreatment of poor American children should be the human rights issue of our time.

Immigration

IN ORDER FOR PEOPLE TO REGAIN CONFIDENCE IN OUR GOVERN-ment, they must see the government confronting some of the major issues facing our country today. Immigration is one of them.

To the media and in the political arena, the word "immigration" now encompasses every person who has migrated to this country, whether illegally or legally. And if you're a Republican who dares to express concerns about the millions of undocumented people in the country, the left automatically slaps you with the label "racist." In order to solve our immigration issues, we must recognize that the two—legal and illegal immigrants—are separate, and both must be dealt with in a strict but humane way.

Solving the immigration issue is an economic and national security issue; it's also one of the most highly charged, politicized issues we face today. If it can be solved, it will close yet another division between the political parties and the American public. But first, as with so many issues, Americans have to come to grips with the faults and shortcomings on both sides. When it comes to illegal immigration, let's be blunt: both parties have utterly failed us. Big business, corporate Republicans love the cheap labor, while Democrats use immigrants as a political wedge in the short-term, holding out for a massive influx of new voters in the long-term.

Americans want solutions, but the loudest voices are the most extreme. The far left wants open borders and sanctuary cities. The far right wants to round up and deport millions of people. Let's be clear: we are talking about families who have been here for generations, including grandparents, mothers, and fathers, as well as young adults brought here as children. Many of these people are as American as apple pie. You know them. They're your neighbors. They work with you. They sit next to you at church. They attend local community events with you. Some of the kids and young adults don't even speak the family's native language, only English. They are your local high school star athletes or valedictorians. So many are productive members of society, minus the proper legal status.

This issue affects every state in America. Depending on how it's handled, it can make or break economies in certain communities, and for some families, it can mean the loss of a mother or father through deportation, someone who, by the way, has been in the country for decades.

As passionate and angry as both sides get on this issue, it is not a hopeless cause. We know what the overwhelming majority of the country does not want. Most Americans do not want open borders. They also reject massive round-ups, internment camps, and deportation. Americans want a practical solution to keep good, productive members of society in the country.

A comprehensive, yet not overly complicated solution could look like this: First, secure the border, whatever it takes. And as redundant as these next statements sound, they have to be said, given today's rhetoric. Legal immigration must be the only path of immigration. Illegal immigration should be illegal and not tolerated. People have to come here legally.

It strikes me how often we hear Democrats, such as House Speaker Nancy Pelosi and Senator Elizabeth Warren, pointedly criticize President Trump, saying, "No one is above the law." When it comes to illegal immigration though, meaning people who have broken the law, what's left unsaid is: "Well, we don't mean them." Our country is dependent on the rule of law to uphold our freedoms; this type of contradiction simply does not work.

Second, allow those who have been here illegally the chance to become permanent legal residents if they have a clean, arrest-free record. Those here illegally should acknowledge that they broke the law, and rather than pay a fine, every adult should be required to perform a number of hours of approved, locally administered community service. It is a sanction we use for numerous other legal violations.

Third, pass what's known as DACA, the Deferred Action for Childhood Arrivals. Children brought here as minors have no culpability for having broken the law. This legislation should make them full legal residents of the United States, unless they have broken the law while living here.

Fourth, eliminate sanctuary cities. With no risk of deportation for immigration violations, there is no longer any need for them.

Fifth, create an earned path to citizenship for adults. Serving honorably in our military or working as a first responder for a certain number of years could earn citizenship. This path could also include years of proven service to your community as a volunteer firefighter, sports coach, teacher's aide, hospital volunteer, etc. The list is endless, so long as it is approved and monitored.

Democrats gain the legalized status they want, a path to citizenship for adults here illegally, and the passage of DACA. Republicans get border security, no amnesty, and an end to sanctuary cities. Most importantly, the American people get a solution that works.

The extremes lose. The American people win. Congress shows that our country is not "a nation divided against itself" but one able to govern successfully.

Welfare and Dependency

WHEN LEFTISTS HEAR THE WORDS "WELFARE REFORM," THEY translate that into something like "racist Republican policy." It's a testament to the nation's perception of the Republican brand today, but it also shows how the Democratic Party has moved further left.

Check out this quote. If a president used words like this today, he or she would be decried as a racist. But…this was Bill Clinton, a Democrat, back in 1996.

Today the Congress will vote on legislation that gives us a chance to live up to that promise, to transform a broken system that traps too many people in a cycle of dependence to one that emphasizes work and independence, to give people on welfare a chance to draw a paycheck, not a welfare check.

When I took office, one out of eleven New Yorkers was on welfare. That is an enormous number.

The reactions on both sides to the large welfare state are typical. Republicans react with horror, calling anyone on welfare a freeloader, someone who costs taxpayers billions. Democrats take a different approach. They patronize people. "These poor [meaning ignorant] people [meaning constituents] can't take care of themselves [meaning shouldn't have to work], so we need to help [meaning give them stuff]."

When I was in office, I looked at it completely differently. Over the previous years, politicians had created a system that trapped people into government-created dependency. Good, intelligent, and capable people calculated that it was in their self-interest to be on welfare instead of working or trying to find a job. Decades of liberal policy left New Yorkers, as well as millions around the nation, stuck on welfare because it was the easiest and most lucrative option for them. They had more money and benefits being on welfare than if they had been working. Sadly, the welfare state degenerated from a hand up to a handout, and generations of families had become accustomed to government dependency as a way of life. For years, liberal policy encouraged dependency over self-reliance.

When I got into office, we immediately began reforms by requiring people who received government assistance to actively seek a job and get to work, and if they couldn't find work, we would provide it. It worked really well. But our success in transforming the welfare state came from doing so much more. We changed the dynamic to make it in someone's self-interest to take that first job by offering an umbrella of security—health-care benefits, day care, and refundable tax credits.

A year later, the federal government ended up passing similar legislation.

While many states offer health care to kids whose families are just above the Medicaid level, we expanded that dramatically and added a new program for adults, offering health care to low-income, working adults who earned too much to qualify for Medicaid but didn't have the resources to buy health coverage. It was essentially free. So, people who took that first job would not have to worry about whether they or their kids had health care, because they had it. Nor did people have to worry about hiring someone to watch their kids. We took care of that, too.

We had nonprofits create day-care slots and after-school programs, and the state funded them. The state's economy was booming with low taxes, a positive regulatory climate, and consistent conservative policy, and that meant more job openings for working mothers and fathers, who could now get the support they needed when it came to their kids.

We also dramatically expanded the earned income tax credit. This meant that workers kept more money in their pockets. So, even if they were working a low-paying job, it was still more lucrative than getting a welfare check.

I vowed to change the paradigm. Having grown up among people of all classes, including many who were poor, I empathize with and believe in people whose families are dependent on welfare. They want to work. They want the pride and dignity that comes with bringing home a paycheck. But the state's welfare system was stacked against them. We changed that.

For the first time in generations, getting a job became something that was in an individual's best economic interest. It created value in people's lives, economically and emotionally.

Every single person has value and abilities. We need to empower people with choices that offer opportunities. These choices make individuals, and for that matter our nation, stronger and more confident. When people can control their own lives, they are no longer dependent on what a government bureaucrat dictates day after day. On a personal level, bringing home a paycheck develops a sense of self-worth, as opposed to sitting at home and getting a government check.

We changed government policy to actually empower low-income people with the chance to live independent, upwardly mobile lives. The policy took the power out of the hands of placating politicians who wanted only to feel good about themselves and not really even help the poor.

This type of policy came naturally to me because I had lived through it. In Peekskill, I grew up with a sort of strange dichotomy. I lived on the outskirts of the city on a dirt road on a farm, where we had a horse and wagon. Remember, this was the mid-1950s. We were truly rural outliers. In nearby downtown, there were high-rise, low-income federal housing projects, home to largely African Americans. The buildings were only half a mile away, so I had this broad exposure to people from all walks of life who faced a myriad of challenges. I witnessed my black friends experience racist behavior. I watched the daily challenges that minorities and whites faced together while living in poverty. Through it all, I never formed an elitist view that some people couldn't take care of themselves so the government had to take care of them. My friends, who came from all sorts of socioeconomic backgrounds and ethnicities, were like everybody else. Some of them were brilliant and motivated, and some of them were lazy.

It led me to *not* see things from a clichéd "those people" standpoint but instead to see people as individuals. As a lawmaker, when I saw welfare dependency, I didn't see a class of people. I saw a family—a father, a mother, and their kids. I asked, "What are we going to do to make their lives better?"

The Democrats created their system, and it created generational dependency. It sapped initiative and self-worth, but the politicians sure felt good about it. They were "taking care of the poor." I always believed that with the right support, the poor could take care of themselves.

On the other hand, the typical Republican solution was to cut everything, with some shrugging their shoulders and saying, "Well, my family was poor, and if we made it, you can too. Good luck." But I saw that we needed a different approach, one that called for the government's actively helping in a way that would create self-interest, success, and independence.

That's my background and my philosophy, and it's why I was able to get so many of these programs through in New York. And in the end, they worked. When I left office, more than one million fewer people were dependent on welfare than when I entered the position. I'm proud of that. More than one million people now had the pride of earning a paycheck and taking part in the American dream, no longer dependent on government.

Communicating

CONSERVATIVES HAVE TO DO A BETTER JOB EXPLAINING HOW THEIR policies work for the benefit of everyone, whether those policies are related to smaller government, legal immigration, or tax cuts.

Republicans have been branded as racists, misogynists, xenophobes, and a slew of other words and phrases not appropriate for this book. Some of the criticism coming from the left, from the media, and in the political arena is unfair and inherent stereotyping. But Republicans, in many ways, brought this on themselves after decades of communicating so poorly to the public. Conservatives fail to tell their story.

Republicans rarely explain how their policies will benefit ordinary, real world, working people. They face everything backward, and it often comes across as selfish, elitist, and greedy. A great example is the cliché, "We're tough on crime!" When a white Republican says that over and over on the campaign trail, what many minority communities unfortunately hear is, "We're gonna lock more of you up!" The way Republicans often explain it, it's as if getting tough on crime will benefit only the person living in a Park Avenue apartment with a doorman or in a gated community. In fact, it's the opposite. Their neighborhoods are safe. We never convey how these policies will benefit the person working at the bodega in Brooklyn at three in the morning or hardworking mothers and fathers in a neighborhood that has taken a bad turn. We fail to explain that we want to be tough on crime because, with the criminals behind bars, they're not going to commit more crimes. It will benefit historically marginalized communities, filled with good people working to make a better life for themselves and their kids.

The fact that a policy has worked logically is one thing, but that's not enough. The policy has to have a positive impact on people's lives—particularly those people who are going to be the most skeptical about those types of policies.

CHAPTER 12

AMERICA IS, AND ALWAYS WILL BE, A SHINING CITY ON A HILL

FOR ALL THE FAILURES OUR COUNTRY HAS HAD OR AREAS IN WHICH we've come up short, America is an amazing nation, unlike any other in history.

Capitalism and the United States get a bad rap with leftists around the world, and that's not just unfair, it's ignorant. Capitalism has lifted more people out of poverty than any other economic system in the history of humanity. Capitalism has created the largest middle class the world has ever seen, all based on a concept America perfected: freedom. America, as the freest nation in the world, socially and economically, has led the way in everything from advancing human rights to creating industries and inventions that make the world a safer and better place, all while remaining a steadfast leader and the envy of the world. America—and capitalism—has done more good for the planet than any other nation at any time in history.

America gets stuff done. We create. We innovate. Ingrained in our DNA is an entrepreneurial spirit, one that few other cultures have. Sure, loads of other countries have had their share of feats. But go to another country and ask virtually any successful businessperson, especially entrepreneurs, how America stacks up to their country when doing business or accomplishing big goals, and they will tell you: America is a place to dream big, go big, and get big things done quickly.

We have ended wars and genocide, conquered the moon, created massive opportunities for our own citizens and countless others around the globe. And we've done so by working together.

It feels good to reflect on stories about President Ronald Reagan and Speaker Tip O'Neill battling over legislation and later having drinks together, or President Bill Clinton joining Speaker Newt Gingrich to pass big-picture policy like welfare reform. The reality is that those people still engaged in severe, bitter partisan fights. But for decades, members of Congress and the public were willing to work together and accept, at a minimum, some degree of compromise.

As a practical matter, if you understand that there are basically two sides on most issues, you can accomplish something, more often than not, by working with the other side. You can accept less than everything you want in a negotiation and still achieve your goal. We do it every day in real life, but in the political world, it has become treasonous. Unfortunately, some on the far left or right deem their own as traitors for working with the other party or making some compromises. Ending up with 80 percent or even half of what was wanted in an end game is sometimes the best solution for the country and our people. Moving forward is often better than walking away.

Pragmatism is rooted in optimism. Pragmatists find solutions and get things done because they're optimistic people. They are not the angry extremists trying to shout down the other side every chance they get. They are open, able, and willing to work together.

Optimism is quintessentially American, built into our frontier spirit and immigrant DNA. Pessimistic naysayers don't hop on boats facing disease and famine or cross deserts and mountains facing starvation and death. You make that journey because you believe—you believe that your destination will provide opportunity and a better life for you and your family.

I know this as a second-generation immigrant. What my father and mother instilled in me comes from generations of immigrants to this country. We understand the value of hard work. We understand that everyone has a different role. And we understand that we all fit into a bigger picture—the idea of America.

There's a big catch here, though. One of the toughest challenges America faces is embracing a concept that sounds simple but has been a problem in all of human history: *tolerance.* You cannot be optimistic about the country and its future while demonizing half the country. Nor can you be pragmatic. You can't even begin to work with people without having tolerance and empathy, a basic understanding of and a respect for others.

> **White lives matter!**
> —Pro-Trump rally attendee, shouting at a Black Lives Matter counter-protester

On September 16, 2017, Trump supporters kicked off the Mother of All Rallies event at the National Mall. Tommy Gunn, neither the adult film actor nor the character in *Rocky V*, organized the event. His name is actually Tom Hodges, but let's face it, Tommy Gunn sounds so much cooler.

With Abraham Lincoln hovering over the scene in his large marble chair, a crowd of Black Lives Matter counter-protesters showed up and began making their way toward Gunn and his pro-Trump group.

The scene got tense. As the counter-protesters got closer, the two sides began shouting at each other. Phones went up, and people began recording, certain they were about to get a violent exchange on video. But as the groups met, something unexpected happened.

Gunn invited Hawk Newsome, the president of Black Lives Matter New York, to come up to the stage and speak to the overwhelmingly white group. Before handing him the microphone, Gunn said, "What we're going to do is something you're not used to, and we're going to give you two minutes of our platform to put your message out." Next, in a very adult moment, unlike the Antifa children on college campuses, Gunn said, "Whether they disagree or agree with your message is irrelevant. It's the fact that you have the right to have the message." He handed the mic to Newsome and told him to go for it.

Even with Gunn alluding to the Constitution in his introduction by saying that Newsome had the right to speak, the crowd was still overtly hostile. Newsome took the mic. Without missing a beat, he launched into his speech in a big, amped-up voice, and he immediately exacerbated the already tense situation. "I am an American. And the beauty of America is that when you see something broke in your country, you can mobilize to fix it." The crowd shrugged, but then he added, "So you ask why there's a Black Lives Matter. Because you can watch a black man die and be choked to death on television and nothing happens. We need to address that."

Jeers! Yells!

"What about black-on-black crime?" someone in the crowd shouted.

Newsome responded, "We are not anticop. We are anti-bad cop. We say if a cop is bad, he needs to get fired like a bad plumber, a bad lawyer, like a bad fucking politician!"

Right then and there, he started to connect with those in the crowd. They erupted in applause. He began to win them over. After all, who doesn't hate politicians?

Newsome then added something else the crowd rallied around: "We don't want handouts; we don't want anything that is yours. We want our God-given right to freedom, liberty, and the pursuit of happiness."

Even more applause, roars, and cheers.

Just as Newsome and the crowd connected, someone shouted out, "All lives matter!"

Maybe it was meant to belittle Newsome; maybe it was a genuine statement to seek dialogue. I don't know, but I know Newsome's response sealed the deal to win over the rest of the people.

"You are so right, my brother; you are so right. All lives matter, right? But when a black life is lost, we get no justice. That is why we say black lives matter. If we really want America great, we do it together."

Once again, the crowd erupted in applause. It was a brief but beautiful moment during a time of hyper-partisanship that has escalated into violent situations at times. Not this time, though. The video of the exchange was picked up by traditional media and in social media, and it went viral with millions of views and positive comments.

This exchange, no matter how small or trivial, is important. It teaches us a basic lesson: when we communicate, we see one another as people—not devils on a hated news network or faceless ghouls hidden behind nameless accounts on social media. When we talk, we find common ground.

It is imperative that we escape our echo chambers in the media, as well as the vats of polluted websites and apps that make up social media. Having contact with people is the essence of being human. This requires empathy, which is unfortunately an old memory, fading day by day.

The lack of will to look at, much less engage with, people on the "other side" has led directly to our current polarized state. This has had and will continue to have disastrous consequences. Now, more than ever, there is a need to reengage in enlightenment, like that of the seventeenth and eighteenth centuries, which emphasized reason and individualism rather than ideology. We need a reawakening in America that values logic and rational conclusions. When people polarize, they pick sides and an ideology, and if the ideology is not on their side, they disqualify it. That prevents logical and rational thought. When we lay out the merits of both sides and come to rational conclusions, as opposed to being constantly mired in ideological partisanship, the vast majority of issues can be solved—or, at minimum, we dissipate the unacceptable vitriol that exists today.

Our politicians need to realize: their side may win an election, but America is not winning the future. If we work together to confront the issues we face, then maybe the American people can return to a belief that the government belongs to us.

CHAPTER 13

WE ARE RESOLVED TO LIBERATE THE SOUL OF AMERICAN LIFE AND PROVE OURSELVES AN AMERICAN PEOPLE IN FACT, SPIRIT, AND PURPOSE

THE POLITICAL FALLOUT FROM THE SEPTEMBER 11 HAUNTS OUR country today. We are in a perpetual state of war abroad, and at home our politicians are failing us.

Did the terrorists win?

It's a heavy question, but it's one that needs to be asked for us to look at where we are today and, more important, where we are going tomorrow.

On January 9, 2002, I gave the first State of the State Address after the attacks:

The spirit of New Yorkers was shown to the world on September 11 and in the days since.

*It is an invincible spirit, a spirit of compassion and courage...
tempered, but not harshened... tested, but not weakened... bent, but
not broken. And because of this spirit, the terrorists have failed.*

*Their goal wasn't just to destroy two towers and kill thousands,
horrible though that was. Their goal was to frighten us, to take away
our freedom and weaken our confidence. They failed. Inspired by the
courage and sacrifice of thousands of New Yorkers, New Yorkers and
Americans are more unified now than we've ever been.*

More unified than ever.

That was then. Now, we are bitterly divided, culturally and
politically.

No. The terrorists did not win, but neither did we.

In Washington, pragmatism has given way to ideology. Ideologues, the most extreme on both sides, are clearly ascendant. The
more outlandish the rhetoric, the more adoration from the base and
media attention. And if you dare work with the other side, you will
be hit with a primary opponent in your next election. The consequences are that nothing gets done.

What has always made America great is that if we have a problem, we solve it. We find a way to get it done, working with anyone
we need to. It's how the American people act, but our government
does not. Politicians have so much ideological baggage, they don't
look for solutions. They look through a political lens, asking, "Does
this line up with my ideology?" If not, then it's off the table!

As for our foreign policy, the War on Terror has no end in sight.
No one can clearly state the end game or what victory would look
like. Our national debt is at an all-time high, and no political party
is addressing it. Our endless wars bring endless bills.

With the Obama administration, it was as if no one had learned
a thing from Iraq about the unintended consequences of over-
throwing dictators. No one learned the dangers of destabilizing
an entire region. Under Obama, we backed the Muslim Brother-
hood against our longtime allies in Egypt. Secretary of State Hillary
Clinton helped overthrow Muammar Gaddafi in Libya, and just

like Iraq, it became a breeding ground for radical Islam. Libya and other nearby countries are now in the same shape Afghanistan was in before 9/11. That country became a lawless training ground for Al-Qaeda to plan, to plot, and to train recruits. Are these newly unstable countries the next staging grounds for another plan to attack America? When will it end?

With our military spread so thin around the world, Iran openly challenges us, clearly working on building nuclear weapons. North Korea's Kim Jong-un openly tests his nukes one day and tries to placate President Trump the next. Russia covertly pushes for civil war in the US.

Russia, in particular, took note of our divisions at home and found deeply sinister ways to take advantage of them. While the members of the public debate the effect that Russian hackers had on the 2016 election, what they're missing is the openly brazen way the hackers did it. Forget for a second stolen or leaked Clinton emails or collusion. Forget Republican or Democrat. Look at what Russians did on social media.

In the same space where you go to see pictures of your family and friends on Facebook, read tweets from your favorite sports figure, or see obnoxious pictures of food on Instagram, Russian state operatives went in and created fake social media accounts that weren't even directly associated with a political party. They went left, right, and everywhere in between to do everything they could to agitate and anger people from all walks of life. They used race, religion, Black Lives Matter, the NRA, Obama, Trump, Hollywood celebrities, and more. Russians antagonized different sides of the political spectrum, working to pit people against one another. Like fools, hundreds of thousands of Americans bought into the propaganda and misinformation and started attacking each other.

Our country's division was once an exception; now division is a demand from each side, politically and culturally. People have picked sides, and if you're not on their side, you're more than part of the problem—*you are the enemy.*

For generations, America remained united through world wars, assassinations of beloved figures, terror attacks, and natural disasters. We looked toward the future optimistically. Now we can't even see straight because we're seething in anger at the guy next door who votes for a different political party.

It is now incumbent upon us, the American people, to allow this no longer.

A nation became a neighborhood.

When I said that at the Republican National Convention of 2004, I had high hopes and aspirations for our country. I thought we could use 9/11 as a turning point to unite us like never before. But as I've written, and as the years have shown us, we did the opposite.

A nation became a neighborhood. We were all New Yorkers.

Sure, for a few days Chicago recognized that real pizza was thin, not a thick Midwest casserole. For a bit, people in Los Angeles realized that New York was a much better city with a far better lifestyle, and that seasons are a good thing. Europe conceded that New York had the best restaurants. And the world recognized that New York City is the best city on the planet for sports.

But more than that, for about a year, throughout the country, we were united. We were patriots.

From the mountains, to the prairies, to the oceans white with foam, people recognized how blessed they were to be in America and how blessed they were to be Americans.

Our country needs to reclaim the sense that we are all in this together; we all share a common future. As a nation of pioneers and immigrants, the future is ingrained in our DNA. America and its people, not always bonded by common backgrounds, languages, or bloodlines, have remained united in the idea of America. We are a community striving toward a better tomorrow, regardless of what separates us—race, religion, or political ideology. And our tomorrow, our future, is a beacon of freedom, opportunity, and endless possibilities.

We need to restore our belief that it is *our* government—our government collectively. We need to restore our belief that Washington can come together to solve problems, not with ideological solutions but by working together and yes, by compromising.

Some of you reading this—conservative or liberal—may get frustrated with the critiques or solutions I've laid out in this book. But I have never considered an elected official an enemy because of an "R" or a "D" next to his or her name. I've never viewed fellow Americans as enemies because they believe in a different philosophy than I do. I hope you don't either.

Only as a unified country can we share a vision of what our future may be. Then, we must work to achieve it. America has always been about the future, never about yesterday. America is still the future and can remain the leader for hundreds of years to come if we recapture our sense of unity, understanding we share a common future. It will start with the leadership of our president and other elected leaders. When it does, hopefully leaders in everything from academia, to media, to local communities will follow, and they will do so by focusing on our commonalities, not political divides.

When you break it down, what we all want is pretty simple: a secure future, safety, a solid education for our kids, job opportunities, and a healthy environment. Most important, we want to live in a community where we have a sense that we are part of the greater whole.

While my reflections on our country's current situation may seem pessimistic, let there be no question: I am optimistic about America's future. We have been through worse and always risen to greater heights. I believe in America, its great people, and its promise. If we work together, we can all reclaim that belief as well.

Even with all the hyper-partisanship, intense anger, and frustration, America is as strong as ever. If our country and leaders address the serious domestic and foreign policy challenges we face, and if they can put aside the toxic partisanship, then Americans will believe in government again.

If you ask average Americans how their lives are—and you exclude the politics of Washington, DC—you'd find that most people are not only optimistic, but they're pretty darn happy.

The country is doing well; the politics of it are failing.

This is why it is so important for our country to mandate that our federal government return to being *of the people, by the people, and for the people,* as President Lincoln and our founding fathers envisioned. If the elected politicians in DC can get out of their bubble and start serving the people rather than their own interests, the United States can and will continue to do great things at home, be a positive influence abroad, and remain the "shining city upon a hill," as President Reagan so eloquently called it.

To the politicians, political elites, and pundits, and to all of those who seek to divide us while waging war for their own interests, I urge you to take a short ride up New York Harbor. To the left, you'll see the Statue of Liberty, the most recognized symbol of freedom in the world, holding her torch high. She welcomed tens of millions of people to our shores, not to become Republicans or Democrats but to pursue a better life as Americans. To the right, you'll look up and see another symbol of freedom, the Freedom Tower itself, soaring 1,776 feet high. That architectural marvel proudly displays our ability to rise from a terrible disaster to greater heights, not as Republicans or Democrats but as Americans. After that, you could walk a few short, boisterous city blocks, arriving at the peaceful, tree-covered area of the 9/11 memorial, engraved with the names of the thousands murdered in the attacks. The civilians and first responders who made the ultimate sacrifice that day responded not as Republicans or Democrats but as Americans. While paying your respects, you'll see a vibrant community full of culture and full of life in every direction, bound together economically and socially. You'll see what Americans can do when we stand together beyond the great divide as we did after September 11, not as Republicans or Democrats but as Americans.

Maybe, just maybe, this would make those who work to divide us see the true beauty in how strong America is when we are united. And for those in elected office, maybe they could realize that their job is to serve the people, not their party.

I hope this country will inspire a new generation of leaders to shine, seeing past the pettiness, silliness, and negativity pervading politics today. If they do, they can bridge the gap in our great divide and become the next great generation, one to lead our country into a new era filled with promise.

They can reignite the torch of freedom so that it burns bright, highlighting the hope, optimism, and welcoming arms America has offered century after century.